ELECTIONS

HELICON

Baltimore—Dublin

in the Church

by Joseph O'Donoghue

The author wishes to thank Mr. Joseph Caulfield of Helicon Press for his many helpful suggestions during the preparation of the manuscript. He also wishes to thank his fellow priests of the Archdiocese of Washington for their friendship and their comments.

Helicon Press, Inc., 1120 N. Calvert St., Baltimore, Md. 21202

Helicon Limited, 20 Upr. Fitzwilliam St., Dublin 2, Ireland

Library of Congress Catalog Card Number 66-26480

Nihil Obstat: Brendan Lawlor
                  Censor Deputatus

Imprimatur: ✠ Robert F. Joyce
                  Bishop of Burlington
                  July 26, 1966

The *Nihil Obstat* and *Imprimatur* are official declarations that a book or pamphlet is considered to be free of doctrinal or moral error. No implication is contained therein that those who have granted the *Nihil Obstat* and *Imprimatur* agree with the contents, opinions or statements expressed.

Printed and bound in the United States of America

TABLE OF CONTENTS

List of Abbreviations

CC—Constitution on the Church
CDR—Constitution on Divine Revelation
CSL—Constitution on the Sacred Liturgy
DCC—Decree on the Catholic Churches of the Eastern Rite
DCE—Declaration on Christian Education
DCP—Decree Concerning the Pastoral Office of Bishops in the Church
DMA—Decree on the Church's Missionary Activity
DMS—Decree on the Media of Social Communication
DOA—Decree on the Adaptation and Renewal of the Religious Life
DOE—Decree on Ecumenism
DOL—Decree on the Laity
DOR—Declaration on the Relation of the Church to Non-Christian Religions
DPL—Decree on the Priestly Life and Ministry
DPT—Decree on Priestly Training
DRF—Declaration on Religious Freedom
PCC—Pastoral Constitution on the Church in the Modern World

ELECTIONS IN THE CHURCH

INTRODUCTION TO A CRISIS

Reports that the Catholic Church is in a state of crisis are rather common these days. What the crisis is and what it means often depends on who is reporting the crisis.

To those holding authority in the Church a *crisis of authority* frequently refers to their intense concern over a lack of docility and obedience within the ranks. To others a crisis of authority means an equally sincere concern about the authoritarian manner and domineering tactics sometimes evidenced in the ecclesiastical administration.

A *crisis of faith* is reported by those who see a drastic reduction in the convictions of the faithful due to the questioning of formerly rigid norms of belief and conduct. For others the crisis of faith is the problem of millions of statistical Catholics who neither comprehend nor care about their purely nominal faith. A *crisis of preservation* has occurred for a minority intent on retaining a traditional deposit which they view as being diminished under a liberalizing movement within the Church. And for those who are intent upon establishing the relevance of the Church to modern man there is a *crisis of relevance*.

The great revealer of crisis within the Church was Vatican II. In the wider perspective of history the Council may be visual-

11

ized someday as the public platform for an inevitable clash of opposing interpretations of what the Church's response should be to the various crises confronting it in modern times. A century from now it may become clear that during the pontificate of Leo XIII the Catholic Church began to experience an ideological renaissance which was to find its eventual expression in Vatican II. In this period there was a frequently frustrated but steady growth of biblical scholarship and of a Bible-centered theology within the Church. This was paralleled by liturgical advances in the knowledge of earlier patterns of worship and in a certain limited adaptation of liturgical practice to the contemporary environment. The continuation of Leo XIII's concern for social issues was producing a hard core of social thought regarding the Church's response to the problems of modern society. Catholic scholarship had begun probing efforts to reassess the role of the Church in the world and its effectiveness in communicating its message. As a result there was evolving within the Church a growing awareness of the need for reform and the directions it could take.

Yet prior to Vatican II this renaissance had not seriously affected the practices of the Church. The daily life of the Church continued in its traditional pattern with only occasional modifications introduced by the relatively small number of administrators who had been influenced by the new learning. On an official level the new learning and the new attitude it provoked was even resisted and its communication impeded by those who felt that it threatened the Church's traditional mission.

It is interesting to speculate on what would have happened if Vatican II had not been summoned. Would the forces of reform and renewal have permeated eventually into the mainstream of Catholic life without the public platform provided by the Council? In the absence of a conciliar assembly could the Church's official administration have continued its policy of containment into the indefinite future? Or would there eventually have been an open clash within the Church leading to disunity and possible schism?

We will never know. Providentially the forces of reform and the forces of preservation met in public debate with the retention of charity and the achievement of consensus.

Vatican II did not solve the recognized crises within the Church or even reduce the tensions within its membership. Its initial accomplishment was rather to publicize the various crises and clarify the tension, thereby bringing the full attention and energy of the Church's membership to its modern problems. To the multiple crises facing the Church it offered neither omniscient formulas nor anathemas. Instead it adopted an open attitude and drafted documentary guidelines for the implementation of the collective wisdom of the universal body.

Thus the Church can expect to remain in a state of growing crisis for some time to come. Tension was provoked by the direct and publicized encounters of opposing views within the Council, in place of previous indirect and unpublicized encounters. That tension can be expected to increase as the faithful themselves begin to debate the great issues. The general feeling of optimism among Catholics as the Church dramatically discovered new sources of enthusiasm and energy deep within its structures will be somewhat mitigated by a growing sense of insecurity as the old sacrosanct ways are questioned and the new and unfamiliar is introduced. The placidity and the certainty of pre-conciliar days will become for many a memory of a better era.

In addition there will be an unfamiliar pressure placed upon every member of the Church because of the Council's professed intent to revitalize Catholicism. World opinion will be closely observing the Church. We have made promises to mankind and we have raised great hopes on international order, social justice and the activation of Christian concern for the world. The conciliar documents have specifically stated an impressive list of expectations.

In the *Constitution on the Church* we have presented a magnificent vision of the Church as the family of God, in which every member contributes his efforts and his wisdom to the benefit of the entire family of God and to the improvement of all mankind. The *Decree on Ecumenism* represents the greatest single Catholic advance in four hundred years in efforts directed toward ending the scandal of Christian division. Eventual reunion has become a possible if distant goal, and action in that direction will be expected. In the *Constitution on the Liturgy* we have emphasized the necessity of a proper pattern of worship. We have established a guideline potentially capable of renewing the inner lives of millions. The *Constitution on the Church in the Modern World* has emphatically declared that the Church must be relevant. We have indicated what the Church should be and what Christians should do.

It is not pleasant to contemplate the possibility of a collective failure to fulfill these expectations. But it could happen. The success—or failure—of Vatican II is still in the future. In the long view of history, the Council will be a success only if its theoretical statements are transferred from paper to reality.

Serious attention should be given to the fact that the conciliar documents *propose* with the understanding that the faithful will *react* or *implement*. The reaction or implementation may take various forms, for example, the establishment of structures providing an affective coordination of charismatic energy, the development of a deeper insight into the theology of the Church and the Christian commitment, and the vigorous stimulation of ecumenical activity. Whether or not Vatican II is a success depends ultimately on the success of these efforts at implementation made by the entire Church, clergy and laity working together.

It will be a difficult process. There is no historical precedent to serve as a guide. Imagination, initiative and multiple experimentation will be needed to determine the best methods of implementation and realization. Without these efforts Vatican II could conceivably become a purely theoretical effort at reform never fully adopted by the Church.

It is not likely that this failure would be due to apathy or lack of concern for reform. Enthusiasm within the Church is high and the conciliar documents have been published, distributed and commented upon at length. But there is the distressing historical record of the formal proposals of earlier councils which failed to achieve the expectation of those who formulated them. As Bishop G. Emmett Carter of London, Ontario, has stated:

> Make no mistake, Vatican II can still fail . . . if the bishops of the world go home and act like office managers, looking to a Roman bureaucracy for every detail and directive, fearful of initiative and happiest when reading instructions sealed with curial arms, then the Constitution on the Church and the decree on bishops and their administration will fall into disuse. And let us not blame the Curia for moving into a vacuum which we will have created.
>
> And if a combination of foot-draggers and gun-jumpers turn the Constitution on the Liturgy into wearying reluctance or a horror of immature experimentation . . . if the laity either decide that it was more comfortable submerged, or if on emerging, they forget that Christ did give special power to teach, govern and sanctify to the apostles and to the bishops their successors, or if they—and some of the priests—forget the power of Holy Orders, the schemata on the laity and on the priesthood, beautiful and moving though they be, are "sound and fury signifying nothing."[1]

Thus it is a distinct possibility that Vatican II could fail through the lack of specific follow-up action within a definite period. It would seem reasonable to predict that the failure to achieve an approximate facsimile of the conciliar promises

1. Cf. the *Canadian Register,* Dec. 11, 1965.

within the next five years could have disastrous effects. The energy and the progressive momentum released by Vatican II could be slowed and then indefinitely stalled as the Council became identified as a purely theoretical discussion of the Church frequently ignored in its day-to-day life. Unless within the present decade there is established a consistent and definite pattern of step-by-step application of the Council's proposals to Church life we may expect a crippling cynicism as millions begin to compare Christian documents with Christian practices.

A collective failure to implement the conciliar teachings would not cancel certain basic achievements of the Council. The documents in themselves are monumental accomplishments in their vision, their concerns, and their optimism. The open discussion of Church life in Vatican II will have far-reaching effects. Too much has been said on the Council floor and in the periods between sessions to permit a return to the pre-conciliar situation and attitude.

But the failure to implement what the Council has said would quietly erode the basis of future Church growth and development within our lifetime. Tension within the Church would quickly climb to the pessimistic and do-nothing level as the difference between magnificent opportunity and meager accomplishment became more apparent. The loss of obvious opportunities to apply Christianity to modern life according to guidelines established by the Council would reduce zeal and enthusiasm among dedicated Christians. We could expect the silent exodus of the talented from active participation in the life of the Church as the Church became less capable of utilizing their ability in its mission. To non-Christians and even to millions of statistical Christians the Church would appear as an institution with only peripheral relevance to their affairs. Perhaps the greatest opportunity ever presented to the Church would have been irretrievably lost.

To make Vatican II a success the Spirit which guided the

Council through so many difficult stages should be recognized as constantly sustaining the post-conciliar efforts of the faithful. So comprehensive are the reforms proposed by Vatican II and so complex are the situations in which they must be applied that the thoughts and suggestions of thousands of involved Christians are necessary to insure a successful implementation. The Council's teaching that the faithful possess charisms, or unique spiritual gifts bestowed by the Spirit for the advantage of the entire Church, must be recognized as operative in the process of devising appropriate methods of implementation of Vatican II. To assign the task to a select few, or even, apathetically, to permit it to be performed by a few, is to court disaster by ignoring the multiple endowment of the Spirit's gifts within the Church. The responsibility for reform belongs equally to all members of the Church. As Cardinal Suenens has remarked, "You lay people, you sisters, you priests, tell us about your Church. We are listening for you to tell us. There has to be more dialogue."

This book is one contribution to the dialogue that can be expected in the process of exploring the possibilities of implementing Vatican II. Its basic contention is that, 1) the great crisis in the Church at this time is a crisis of specifically implementing Vatican II, and 2) that the utilization of the elective process will be a significant factor in developing the communication and the shared wisdom necessary to resolve this crisis and the related crises confronting the Church.

The elective process has traditionally been the method employed by the people of God both to provide candidates for the various ministries of the Church and to indirectly determine the direction of Church affairs by entrusting leadership to those whose policy and attitude had previously reflected the consensus of the membership. The modern confinement of the use of elections to a relatively small number of electors selecting candidates for only a certain number of offices in the Church should not obscure the fact that a far different tradition prevailed throughout the greater period of Church history. In his monumental work on the role of the laity in the Church, Yves Congar repeatedly refers to the principle that whenever the Church has ordered its own life freely and in accordance with its own genius the whole community has been active both in the elective and the directive function.

> "Choose your men," say the Apostles, "and we will appoint them" [Acts 6:1-3]. Not a single ancient text shows anything but a designation of the best fitted person in which all the people collaborate, and a collation to sacred powers which is the business of the episcopate alone. . . .
>
> The participation of laity, especially of rulers, was regarded as an essential feature of great councils from the Latern in 1215 to Trent inclusive, when they became essentially councils for reform and, more generally, councils of Christendom, assemblies to ensure unanimity—and so effectiveness—for decisions concerning crusades, the peace of the Christian commonwealth, or some work for the wellbeing of the Church. The widest possible representation of the different "estates" and corporations, of the chief sovereign or feudal powers, seemed at that time to be essential to a council and its oecumenicity.[2]

It is significant that the first recorded use of the elective process in the Apostolic Church had the effect of resolving an incipient crisis.[3] The Greek members of the early Church were complaining of a preferential treatment accorded to the Hebrew widows; the entire assembly utilized the elective process to

2. Yves Congar, O.P., *Lay People in the Church* (Westminster: Newman, 1957), pp. 234, 237.

3. Anscar Parsons believes that the earlier (Acts 1:15-26) choice of Matthias was not an election in the proper sense since the assembly of the faithful expressly refrained from a deliberate choice. The preliminary decision to make Joseph Barsabas and Matthias the two candidates could be regarded as the result of some form of election. Cf. Anscar Parsons, O.F.M. Cap., *Canonical Elections, An Historical Synopsis and Commentary* (Washington: The Catholic University of America Press, 1939), p. 9.

determine an impartial group who could be expected to provide justice and good order within the community.

> About this time, when the number of disciples was continually increasing, the Greeks complained that in the daily distribution of food the Hebrew widows were being given preferential treatment. The twelve summoned the whole body of the disciples together, and said,
> "It is not right that we should have to neglect preaching the Word of God in order to look after the accounts. You, our brothers, must look round and pick out from your number seven men of good reputation who are both practical and spiritually-minded and we will put them in charge of this matter. Then we shall devote ourselves wholeheartedly to prayer and the ministry of the Word."
> This brief speech met with unanimous approval and they chose Stephen, a man full of faith and the Holy Spirit, Philip, Prochorus, Nicanor, Timon, Parmenas, and Nicolas of Antioch who had previously been a convert to the Jewish faith. They brought these men before the apostles, and they, after prayer, laid their hands upon them.
> So the Word of God gained more and more ground. The number of disciples in Jerusalem very greatly increased, while a considerable proportion of the priesthood accepted the faith.[4]

At the council of Jerusalem the elective process was again used to prepare the groundwork for the resolution of a difficulty in the early Church, the obligations and status of Gentile converts. Chapter 15 of the Acts of the Apostles indicates that Paul and Barnabas attended the council as representatives selected by the entire Church in Antioch, and that the apostles, the elders, and the whole Church in Jerusalem decided to send Judas and Silas to Antioch as representatives bearing a decision arrived at by common deliberation.[5] The decision regarding the

4. Acts 6:1-7.
5. "Naturally this caused a serious upset among them and much earnest discussion followed with Paul and Barnabas. Finally it was agreed that Paul and Barnabas should go up to Jerusalem with some of their own people

obligation of converts was made by the apostles and elders after an exhaustive inquiry of the views of the delegates.[6]

The Apostolic Church used the elective process to determine the selection of bishops and to support their right to the ministry on the basis of the collective consent given to their election. Pope St. Clement I refers to the role of general consent in the life of the Church in the period immediately following the death of the last apostle.

> Our apostles also knew, through our Lord Jesus Christ, that there would be strife on account of the office of the episcopate. For this reason, therefore, inasmuch as they had obtained a perfect knowledge of this, they appointed those ministers already mentioned, and afterward gave instructions that when these should fall asleep, other approved men should succeed them in the ministry. We are of the opinion that those appointed by them, or afterwards by other eminent men, *with the consent of the whole Church* . . . cannot be justly dismissed from the ministry.[7]

The general rules for the election of bishops in the early Church are evident from the Canons of Hippolytus, the Apostolic Constitutions, and the correspondence of St. Cyprian. Elements common to the elective establishment of bishops included the recommendation of the clergy, the vote of the people and the consent of neighboring bishops.[8] But the elective process was also used to determine other offices of the Church. In the African Church of the third and fourth centuries there

---

to confer with the apostles and elders about the whole question" (Acts 15:2).

"Then the apostles, the elders and the whole Church agreed to choose representatives and send them to Antioch with Paul and Barnabas. Their names were Judas, surnamed Barsabas, and Silas, both leading men of the brotherhood" (Acts 15:22).

6. Acts 15:6.

7. *Epistola Clementis*, I, 44.

8. Cf. "Election des évêques" in *Dictionnaire de théologie catholique*, p. 2256.

were *laici seniores* elected by the people and holding an office intermediate between the hierarchy and ordinary laymen. These lay officials apparently formed an administrative board assisting the bishop and, with the bishop, collectively constituted a court of judgment in certain affairs.[9]

The use of the monastic movement both reflected and intensified the elective and representative aspects of early Church life. The sixth century Rule of St. Benedict directed that the abbot be elected by the monks of the community[10]; the rule of Caesarius of Arles of approximately the same period prescribes that the nuns in each monastery elect the abbess.[11] In the seventh century, under the influence of Pope Gregory the Great, the papacy strongly endorsed the freedom of the monasteries by several decrees favoring the free election of superiors by the members of the particular congregations.[12] This practice eventually contributed to the Church's common law the concept of a fixed electoral body responsible for various types of election.[13] Thus Bernard of Pavia, writing at the close of the twelfth century, could describe election as a general method of summoning a person to an ecclesiastical office, whether a monastery, a bishopric or the benefice of a collegiate church, by those immediately concerned.[14] By the thirteenth century the universities of Paris and Oxford were regulating their own affairs through the use of elective and representative procedures in which clergy and laity participated jointly.[15] In the same period

9. Cf. P. G. Caron, *Revue Internationale des Droits de L'Antiquité,* Vol. VI (1951), pp. 7-22.

10. *Regula Monachorum,* Chap. 44.

11. Parsons, *Canonical Elections,* p. 29.

12. Cf. Jean Harduin, *Acta Conciliorum et Epistolae Decretales Ac Constitutiones Summorum Pontificum,* Vol. III, p. 538.

13. Parsons, *Canonical Elections,* p. 38.

14. Cf. Bernadus Papiensis, *Summa Decretalium* (Ratisbon, 1860), p. 307.

15. Cf. H. Rashdall, *The Universities of Europe in the Middle Ages,* ed. F. M. Powicke and A. B. Emden, 3 vols. (Oxford: The Clarendon Press, 1936).

many churches were being built and maintained by elected representatives of the laity.[16]

And yet the elective process and the related factor of lay representation in ecclesiastical affairs did not possess an assured status in the medieval Church. Although the ancient ecclesiastical election of a bishop by the clergy and people with the cooperation and consent of neighboring bishops remained the general law of the Church until the twelfth century, there were various factors in medieval society which tended to impede its implementation.[17] The principle formulated by Pope Celestine I[18] and repeated by Pope Leo I in the fifth century—that no city is to be forced to take a bishop if he has not been freely chosen by clergy and people—continued to be restated by local synods such as that of Paris in 829.[19]

But in practice powerful nobles frequently exercised predominant influence in the election of bishops and other ecclesiastical office holders within the area of their immediate control.[20] When in 1122 the Concordat of Worms successfully concluded almost a century of effort by popes such as Leo IX, Nicholas II and Gregory VII to secure free elections to ecclesiastical offices, their collective efforts could be interpreted as having freed the Church from royal interference in the elective process.[21] But the achievement could also be interpreted as encouraging an elimination of lay involvement in the direction of Church life.

> Pope St. Gregory VII's reform restored the old discipline for a time; but eventually it became necessary to protect the independence of the ecclesiastical order against the

16. Cf. Francis Aidan, Cardinal Gasquet, *Parish Life in Medieval England* (London: Methuen & Co., 1906).
17. Parsons, *Canonical Elections,* pp. 40 ff.
18. Celestine I, *ep. IV,* 5.
19. Cf. Harduin, *Acta Conciliorum,* Vol. IV, pp. 1289 ff.
20. Cf. "Election des évêques," pp. 2265 ff.
21. Cf. Parsons, *Canonical Elections,* p. 46.

princes by making the nomination to bishoprics a purely clerical affair. Election by cathedral chapters eliminated the other clergy, as well as the laity. Moreover the Holy See increasingly asserted rights of intervention, confirmation and even direct nomination; by the beginning of the thirteenth century it was reserving to itself nomination to all benefices, a process completed by the Avignon popes, with deplorable results in the fiscal field. The old tradition, then, wherein the Church spontaneously regulated her life in such a way as actively to involve the whole community, each according to his condition, was brought to an end by powerful laymen abusing their position.[22]

The Church's defensive reaction to the reformation tended to further diminish the reliance on an elective process involving clergy and laity. The Council of Trent drafted important legislation concerning the elections of religious and nuns (for example, the secret ballot),[23] and these prescriptions had their influence on the general law of elections wherever observed. But after the Council of Trent there were no important developments of the elective process.[24]

The cathedral chapter, whose members in the eleventh and twelfth centuries had been collaborators with the bishop and whose consent had been necessary for the administration of temporal affairs, became a venerable relic with no appreciable responsibility and only a ritualistic function.[25] The practice of electing bishops also declined.

The election of a bishop, which had been the typical canonical election in decretal law, became the rare exception during the period after the Council of Trent. In the United States as elsewhere the selection of candidates for the episcopacy changed with the growth of the Church. Bishop

22. Congar, *Lay People*, p. 233.
23. Session XXV.
24. Cf. Parsons, *Canonical Elections*, p. 69.
25. Cf. Tomas Garcia Barberena, "Collegiality at Diocesan Level: The Western Presbyterate" in Vol. 8 of Concilium (Glen Rock, N. J.: Paulist Press, 1966), p. 27.

Carroll by special concession of the Holy See was nominated by the local clergy. Others were chosen at the suggestion of their Metropolitan and fellow suffragans and some had their names presented by individual bishops. From 1884 to 1916 the hierarchy of the United States as well as all Diocesan Consultors and Irremoveable Rectors enjoyed the right of recommending candidates for bishoprics according to a procedure which was somewhat like an election. But these presentations of lists of three names, dignus, dignior, dignissimus, were neither elections nor nominations, but merely recommendations.[26]

Even the accomplishments of Trent regarding the election of religious tended to harden into formal procedures devoid of the freedom generally associated with the elective process. Although Canon law is specific on the method to be followed in ecclesiastical elections,[27] Cardinal Suenens has indicated that the representative nature of elective bodies in religious congregations needs considerable improvement.

A congregation is governed as to ordinary affairs by one of its members, the Superior General, assisted by a Council, and as to extraordinary affairs by the General Chapter. . . .

Representation is often one-sided. This arises from the preponderance of ex officio members over elected members, of Superiors over ordinary members. A certain concept of religious obedience and of what is "suitable" leads a number of religious to send Superiors as delegates to the Chapter rather than choose them principally for their competence, to choose older rather than younger men, and in the case of congregations working in several fields, to overstress one or other of them.[28]

The emphasis placed by Vatican II on the principle of collegiality, or shared responsibility, could be viewed as involving a

26. Parsons, *Canonical Elections*, p. 78.

27. Cf. "Election" in the *New Catholic Encyclopedia* (New York: McGraw Hill, 1967).

28. Leon Joseph Cardinal Suenens, *The Nun in the World* (Westminster: Newman, 1963), p. 154.

revitalization of an elective factor which had become somewhat dormant in recent centuries. In fact the elective process could be a key factor in transferring Vatican II's teaching on collegiality from theory to practice. It seems unlikely that the collegiate structures desired by the council on every level of Church life—parish, diocese, nation and international assembly—will be achieved without the development of specific elective processes determining representative roles.

The elective process has been the traditional means used to consult the wisdom of all the people of God in the selection of the various ministers who serve and guide its collective life. But it would be a serious mistake to consider the elective process as being solely concerned with the selection of ecclesiastical office holders. Of greater importance in the long life of the Church has been the corollary of the elective process, that is, the resulting opportunity for the free exchange of charismatic and prophetic insights occurring within an open structure of leadership selection. The Church cannot be considered as a democracy; pastors of souls are not endowed with the authority of office by democratic procedures.

> Bishops, as successors of the apostles, receive from the Lord, to whom was given all power in heaven and on earth, the mission to teach all nations and to preach the Gospel to every creature, so that all men may attain to salvation by faith, baptism and the fulfillment of the commandments (CC 24).

But neither should the Church be approached as a monarchy; the non-consultative appointment of functions and offices by superior fiat is contrary to both the theology and the historical practice of the Church. What Hans Küng has remarked concerning an ecumenical council would seem to be equally applicable to the general life of the Church.

> In this day and hour of the laity we have become sensitive to the fact that an ecumenical council by human convoca-

tion is a representation of the *Church*, which in equally important proportions (although not important in the same way) consists of *lay persons* as well as officeholders. Therefore a *perfect* representation of the Church also calls for a direct, not only an indirect, representation of the laity. Such a call—as we have seen—is not only important because of the position accorded to the congregation in the New Testament and especially in the account of the "Council of the Apostles," but is likewise supported by the very history of the first Christian synods as well as of the later councils (albeit in a changing degree).[29]

In the course of the Second Vatican Council the reciprocal relation between the development of structures and the advance of theological insights became clear. The council's early use of an elective structure in determining commission members responsible for drafting the conciliar decrees and the practice of encouraging conciliar addresses by speakers representing various groups assisted in the development of the theology of collegiality. In turn, the theological formulation of collegiality in the conciliar documents contributed to the subsequent development of elective structures within episcopal conferences and the international synod of bishops.

The same process can be expected on various levels of Church life in the post-conciliar era. For example, the development of structures of shared responsibility in parish life will assist in the development of a theology of the parish which will in turn contribute to the further development of structures concretizing theology in the daily life of the Church.

> The laity should be able to make themselves heard by the ecclesiastical authorities, by way of information or advice, in everything that concerns them or wherein they may be able to make a useful contribution. . . .
> That ancient institution the parish began as a living community of men and women, in structure frankly popular and

29. Hans Küng, *Structures of the Church* (New York: Nelson, 1964), p. 215.

democratic, if that anachronistic word be not misleading; within its framework the faithful were concerned in the running of things and had a voice in many decisions. The basic community, religious as well as civil, had a sort of administrative autonomy in everyday life, thanks to a system of self-managing councils and organisms.[30]

It is not easy to be specific in suggesting the particular forms which the elective process may assume in the post-conciliar Church or the ideas which may result from a representative interchange of opinion and insight among all the faithful. But the details of reform are at least as necessary as the theory itself; without some form of specific implementation the collegiality of Vatican II could atrophy into a sterility removed from the invigorating influence of practical realization. The concrete, if brief, treatment of the comprehensive range of Church life which follows is intended as a stimulus in provoking additional thoughts and suggestions—that hopefully will lead to action—on the specific implementation of Vatican II in these days of a new Pentecost.

30. Congar, *Lay People*, p. 254.

Chapter One

THE BISHOP IN HIS DIOCESE: GENERAL OR FATHER?

Future generations will probably pay special tribute to the bishops of Vatican II because of their forthright and sincere expression of their own duties. In the *Decree Concerning the Pastoral Office of Bishops in the Church* there are listed norms and general principles which in many instances do not reflect the present policy of the official Church and which consequently place a great deal of pressure upon the bishops to achieve them in their own dioceses. For the first time in the two-thousand-year history of the Church the lower clergy and the laity have a rather specific standard by which to measure the fulfillment—or lack of fulfillment—of the episcopal ideal within their own diocese.

It is possible to view the bishops' official recognition of the need for shared responsibility and communication within their dioceses as an impressive vindication of the pioneering efforts of a North American bishop to establish shared responsibility within his own diocese almost a century and a half before Vatican II. Before considering the conciliar recommendations pertaining to dioceses, let us recall what Bishop John England of Charleston achieved in his diocese in the early decades of the nineteenth century.

1. THE ACHIEVEMENT OF BISHOP ENGLAND

On November 24, 1823 Bishop John England, the priests and lay delegates of the diocese of Charleston adopted in open assembly *The Constitution of the Roman Catholic Church of the Diocese of Charleston*.[1] According to this constitution each parish would have its own board of elected laymen, and each year a convention of these elected lay delegates and their priests would be held under the presidency of Bishop England. As bishop of the diocese John England retained the power proper to him as a successor of the apostles; but the right to regulate the temporal affairs of the Church was entrusted to the faithful. The laymen elected in each parish served as an advisory board to the pastor, and as a corporate board retained title to Church property within the parish subject to the spiritual authority of the bishop. The diocesan convention ("a body of sage, prudent and religious counselors to aid the proper ecclesiastical government of the Church" as Bishop England referred to it) selected a Board of Trustees (5 clergy, 12 laymen) which had the power to dispose of overall diocesan funds. The convention itself consisted of two legislative bodies, a House of Clergy and a House of Lay Delegates, whose acts became effective when ratified by the bishop.

It worked. Bishop England said that the constitution had "produced efforts of cooperation and mutual confidence and affection between our several churches, as well as between the bishop and the churches." The future Pope Gregory XVI, a friend and advisor of Bishop England, endorsed his action: "the wonderful tranquility in the diocese of Charleston is the proof of the wisdom of its bishop."

But it was not imitated. Bishop John England was the only American bishop to share his episcopal responsibility with elected lay delegates. His potential influence upon the rest of

1. For an analysis of Bishop England's Constitution, see George Traynor, "Charter for Laymen, 1822," *Commonweal*, Dec. 18, 1964.

the American Church was reduced by the fact that ecclesiastical politics blocked any possibility of his being elevated to more important dioceses. His death in 1842 brought the twenty-year old constitution and convention to an official close in the American Church. It is somewhat ironical that a close study of conciliar documents and multiple experimentation are now needed to recover what could have been a national inheritance.

It is interesting to speculate on the effects John England could have had on the entire American Church if his pattern of representative contact and communication among bishop, priests and laity had been followed. There would certainly be a closer rapport between bishop and laity than that which now exists.

At a meeting of the South African bishops in Rome, John Cogley remarked that despite his lifelong involvement in apostolic activities within the United States he had never once held a serious conversation with an American bishop. Is this type of isolation between the bishops and a committed layman typical of the United States Church? On the surface it would seem to be a shocking exception to the general rule. A glance at a few issues of the average diocesan newspaper indicates that the bishop is apparently in constant contact with the faithful. He is photographed and quoted at confirmations, commencements, dedications, and banquets with weekly consistency. And everywhere he goes he is surrounded by the faithful.

Yet these contacts are official affairs within an established pattern of encounter that is both ritualized and perfunctory. It frequently happens that the photographs in the diocesan newspapers are carefully staged poses which represent only a quick handshake for most of the participants. For many of the laity (and for many of the clergy as well) the bishop is a distant figure frequently seen on occasions of state but seldom encountered on an informal, personal basis.

Of course no bishop desires a bond with his people which

is merely institutional and impersonal; his own priesthood was originally accepted with the intention of being a father to his people. The present situation should be seen as the result not of individual preference but of inescapable necessities within the present structure. In addition to his traditional round of official appearances and social obligations the average bishop must of necessity spend a great deal of time and energy as general manager and chief builder within a vast organizational structure.

To many Catholics, the large diocese in which they live appears to be a vast bureaucracy with a pyramidical structure, of which they constitute the base. Their view of the diocese could be confirmed by consulting the annual *Official Catholic Directory*, which reports the organizational and statistical pattern of the American Church. The account of each diocese begins with the listing of the bishop and his biography, followed by the names and functions of those officials closest to him in the chain of command, viz. the reverend directors of the various diocesan offices. These appointed clerics occupy the key administerial positions in the diocese (Superintendent of Schools, Director of Catholic Charities, Director of Catholic Youth Organizations, etc.), and collectively constitute what is known as the chancery of the diocese. After their names and offices there appears a list of the parishes and their clergy arranged in alphabetical order. Next the special institutions of the diocese are listed: seminaries, colleges, hospitals, and so forth. The report of each diocese concludes with a compilation of statistics regarding the faithful.

It is obvious that the entire system has many of the sociological qualities and problems of any bureaucracy; there is a series of complex relationships involving some type of communication among members, and a very definite chain of command.[2] In fair-

---

2. "The church is more than a simple society made up of members and officers; it is also a company that employs a full-time staff. This situation gives rise to an employer-employee relationship. On the one hand there are

ness to the system it should be pointed out that it can, and occasionally does, operate as a structure of shared responsibility and mutual communication. Under normal conditions the parish clergy within a diocese can be expected to serve as the eyes and hands of the bishop. By carefully listening to their reports and by balancing their suggestions a bishop is in a position to make those decisions most likely to advance the Church in a changing world.

But there are too many dioceses in which the system fails completely. How can a bishop maintain vital contact with his clergy and faithful in those dioceses with over a thousand priests and hundreds of parishes? How can a pastor deprived of even a consultative share in overall diocesan planning contribute to its effectiveness? And how can a program handed down from on high engage the sympathies of pastors and faithful and meet their real problems?

The customary solution is to rely upon a representative sampling of the clergy who usually occupy chancery positions and who constitute an inner corps of episcopal advisors. Unfortunately there is no guarantee that the inner corps is aware of developments known to the outer corps, or that either corps can see the full picture of the Church's status in the area. The situation is paradoxical in that it is the very success of the Church which multiplies its problems. Due to an annual increase in the number of parishes, a bishop and his chancery advisors may find themselves on the apex of a pyramid from which the view is magnificent but from which very little is heard of the rumblings coming from the foundation.[3]

---

the employers: bishops, pastors, chancery officials, superiors of religious orders, and administrators of church institutions. On the other hand there are the employees: assistant pastors, members of religious communities (priests, brothers, or nuns), and lay employees"—William H. DuBay, *The Human Church* (New York: Doubleday & Company, 1966), p. 177.

3. For a historical perspective of the development of ecclesiastical structures, see *Historical Problems of Church Renewal*, Vol. 7 of Concilium (Glen Rock, N. J.: Paulist Press, 1965).

2. THE FUNDAMENTAL PROBLEM: COMMUNICATION

If the structural problem of the Church in America as now administered could be summarized in a single word, that word would be *communication*.[4] For example, in discussions of ecclesiastical do-nothingism on civil rights it has been customary and perhaps necessary in some instances to focus on the particular decisions of certain prelates. But it is necessary also to focus on the organizational structure responsible for producing a personalized administration isolated from outside counsel. The present structure was designed to facilitate the dispensing of directives from a central source; widespread consultation among clergy and laity is not formally recognized as a value within the system and there is no machinery to receive advice and counsel from sources outside the system. The presumption is that major decisions can be made by officials on the basis of their personal familiarity with the matter under consideration. New developments and alternative proposals reach the decision-making apparatus only on an informal, unorganized basis which cannot adequately indicate their value.

Something similar could be said of the opposition to liturgical and catechetical reforms. The real problem is not that Bishop so-and-so is out of touch with the real world; the prob-

---

4. In November, 1965 a special episcopal committee presented to the American bishops an "Interim Report on the Greater Participation and Involvement of the Laity in the Life and Work of the Church." The report outlines five points as major "difficulties" found in most U. S. dioceses:

1. There are no present structures of formal communications upward in the church.
2. There are "few meaningful" channels of communications downward.
3. These conditions have resulted in "apathy on the part of the majority" of people.
4. There are problems of communication between "a bishop and his pastors, his clergy in general, his 'staff' people."
5. The size of most U. S. dioceses complicates administration and so the need to use the most professional modern systems and methods is "massive and acute."

lem is that the Church is not structured in such a way that effective communication of its collective wisdom can take place. The result is that in many instances the non-communicating Church is simply incapable of flexible response to changing needs.

The absence of effective communication within a diocese has far-reaching effects. It is a sound administrative principle that the effectiveness with which subordinates carry out a decision or a program is in direct proportion to the amount of participation they had in the making of it. A diocese which relies on the postal service to maintain contact with its hundreds of clerical outposts may appear extremely efficient as episcopal orders and chancery directives move steadily from the central office to every rectory. But the absence of a reverse flow of reactions and ideas has its effects. Directives framed in ignorance of the concrete situation with which they deal are often simply inapplicable and therefore are either quietly ignored or radically altered. The general system of decisions without participation (or a semblance of consultation) frequently results in very limited response to even the most solemnly and stringently worded directives. The ecclesiastical rigidity resulting from communication failures of this type could normally be expected to increase in the future. The growth of urban centers will further complicate the problem where it now exists in addition to introducing it in those areas undergoing vast expansion.

3. THE APPOINTIVE SYSTEM

The situation presents an interesting question. Who really is in charge in many of our larger dioceses? It is not an easy question to answer. Is it the bishop whose heavy cycle of ecclesiastical and social functions combined with the endless details of daily financial management dissipate his time and energy? Or are the chancery officials in charge, a corps of specialists in a complex bureaucracy frequently beyond their power to control or even to understand completely? How much effect on decisions comes from the parish clergy, infrequently consulted and rarely involved in the overall management problems?

Perhaps the best answer is that *tradition* is in charge—the customary, established way is the safe way. In some chanceries the general presumption would seem to be that all the answers to major problems have long since been supplied; it is merely a question of recalling previous decisions and patiently applying them again. It is important to re-emphasize that the situation was not designed to operate this way. The Tridentine reforms tended to establish the bishop as a general surrounded by a general staff. In this semi-military complex there is a resultant tendency to regard any criticism as a disloyalty to the commander, and any efforts at innovation as an implicit questioning of the established wisdom.[5]

The extraordinary ability of the system to perpetuate itself despite its weaknesses, recognized by all concerned, may be due to the siege-mentality and military response of the post-Tridentine Church. The system's power to perpetuate itself may also be partially due to the *appointive* promotion system by which power is passed from generation to generation of ecclesiastical officials. In this regard a study of the institutionalized promotion system in chanceries would be most helpful (if it could be made).[6] The *appointive* method of selecting Church officials

5. "The whole New Testament deliberately avoids the secular terms for office (*arché, timé, telos*) where the Christian community is concerned, because all these terms express a dominating attitude"—Hans Küng, "The Charismatic Structure of the Church," in *The Church and Ecumenism,* Vol. 4 of Concilium.

6. "There is, moreover, in any institutionalized promotion system, as an unintended concomitant of the very necessary stability that institutionalization provides, a tendency to reward in some form everything that does not threaten the status quo. . . .

"Some time ago I said to some Catholic sociologists that an important part of any sociological study of institutions was to understand what factors, manifest and latent, affect promotion. When I suggested that this would be a good topic for study in connection with the Church in America, one sociologist who is also a priest agreed but said, 'You'll get into trouble if you try to study that.' Such attitudes speak volumes if they really are repre-

frequently means that the majority of appointees will have gained their position by having previously adopted a program of action in agreement with the established wisdom. Since bishops usually rely on the advice of various chancery officials to fill minor positions in their departments, an incoming chancery official knows who selected him and why. Having been thus honored by the choice of a superior official the new official can be expected subsequently to endorse the wisdom of that superior. Only a serious blunder (perhaps a non-traditional action) would result in his removal from the chancery "team." He can reasonably expect to be promoted eventually to a major position from which in turn he will exercise predominant influence on the selection of minor officials in his department.

Even when the inner corps of episcopal advisers is officially enlarged by the establishment of boards of education, and various commissions, the appointive method of selection has long-range effects. Can effective exchange of views occur among hand-picked members of the board with the episcopal chooser present? And are "appointed" representatives really representative? For example, how open to an effective exchange of opposing views is a diocesan board of education whose members, clergy and laity, are selected by the bishop? Or how responsive to the expressed needs of the faithful is a diocesan official whose tenure in office depends upon his personal relationship with the bishop?

It is true that the appointive system has undeniable benefits. By careful selection a bishop can fill most of the major chancery positions with individuals whose decisions and attitudes will be comparable to his own. At the same time he can be confident that all incipient problems will either be handled in the traditional manner or else directed to his personal attention. And

sentative of large numbers of administrators"—Thomas F. O'Dea, *American Catholic Dilemma* (New York: Sheed and Ward, 1958), p. 136.

under a reasonably perceptive bishop the appointive offices in the diocese are bestowed upon the individuals whose talents are recognized and respected by their peers.

But the appointive system of selecting Church leaders has definite disadvantages, and these are bound to increase at an almost geometric rate during the coming decade. Many dioceses have already expanded both in size and in complexity of problems beyond the capacity of even the most perceptive bishop to exercise the necessary screening of potential candidates prior to appointment. The majority of dioceses in the United States can be expected to follow the same pattern. Any reasonably informed member of the Church can appreciate the fact that the appointive system has frequently resulted in surrounding a bishop with specialists who by reason of their limited background are incapable of collaborating with those of different views. The average bishop would probably prefer to fill certain offices on the basis of a selection by those clergy and laity professionally equipped to pass judgment on the merits of prospective candidates. It would also seem reasonable to suspect that some of the bishops entrusted with the responsibility of recommending an episcopal candidate for a vacant diocese would prefer to compare their judgment with that of clergy and laity competent to make similar recommendations.

4. ANNUAL DIOCESAN ASSEMBLY

One of the providential results of Vatican II was that its enforced absences made it necessary for many bishops to initiate a wider delegation of their individual powers and functions. Especially fortunate is the fact that the implementation of the *Constitution on the Sacred Liturgy* and the *Decree on Ecumenism* have somewhat broadened the range of individuals consulted by a bishop within his diocese. But the moderate success achieved up to now in implementing these decisions of the Council will be considerably more difficult to obtain with the

Constitution on the Church, the document which many think the most important accomplishment of Vatican II.

Several decades of study and limited experimentation had prepared a hardy corps of liturgical pioneers. They were ready to step forward from positions outside the customary power structure of the Church with specific suggestions for implementing the new liturgical constitution. The ecumenical movement had less ground work, but at least it could rely on the example of several outstanding leaders in Catholic, Protestant and Jewish circles. Yet one would look in vain for a single American diocese which in the years prior to Vatican II had achieved anything even remotely resembling the shared power structure of the diocese of Charleston under Bishop John England in the early nineteenth century.

A promising sign for the future is that the experiments necessary to achieve a pattern of shared responsibility are being conducted in a number of dioceses.[7] Optimism, however, is somewhat mitigated by the fact that a relatively small percentage of the American Church is actually involved in the trial of possible structures. Under the leadership of Cardinal Ritter the progressive archdiocese of St. Louis has initiated a program of parish and diocesan assemblies designed to establish a pattern of involvement in which all the faithful can share. A number of other dioceses are similarly engaged in a search for structures permitting maximum participation in the life of the Church.[8]

7. The first diocese in North America to set up a diocesan council patterned after the Second Vatican Council was Sault Ste. Marie in Canada. Every parish in Bishop Alexander Carter's diocese has one or more representatives on various commissions of the diocesan "little council."

8. Cardinal Joseph Ritter has announced that an archdiocesan-wide assembly of elected laymen, religious and priests will be held before the 1967 Archdiocesan Synod. The assembly will discuss and review recommendations to be brought before the synod.—*St. Louis Review,* February 11, 1966.

Archbishop John F. Dearden has announced an archdiocesan goal that would have clergy and laymen operating the church as a partnership. The path to the goal was the subject of eight weeks of person-to-person discus-

But press reports of these developments continually mention the same dioceses; it would seem that less than ten percent of the American dioceses are actually searching for new forms of shared responsibility. A project of such eminent importance deserves to become the recipient of considerable effort on the part of all. What is there to prevent the American Church from reintroducing the practice of a diocesan convention like that initiated by Bishop John England?

It would seem reasonable to expect that an annual diocesan assembly of clergy and elected lay delegates from every parish could be an essential factor in developing a sense of shared responsibility and collective action within a diocese. A carefully planned assembly of perhaps a week's duration could replace today's uneven or non-existent association of apostolic efforts by placing the wide variety of commitments within the context of a collective review and overall coordination. Within an open assembly it would be possible to distill the collective wisdom of the faithful into meaningful decisions and to eliminate unnecessary duplication of efforts. An annual assembly could provide each diocese with the opportunity for a coordination of efforts and a pooling of resources within the various apostolates.

> In the present circumstances, it is quite necessary that, in the area of lay activity, the united and organized form of the apostolate be strengthened. In fact, only the pooling of resources is capable of fully achieving all the aims of the modern apostolate and firmly protecting its interests (DOL 18).

---

sion that Archbishop Deardon held with approximately 120 representative Catholic laymen. Suggestions already decided upon include: a) a synod to be held in Detroit in the Spring of 1967, which would include religious and laity as well as priests; b) election, rather than appointment, of laymen to parish committees; c) establishment of parochial school boards and streamlining of the parochial school system; d) the creation of an archdiocesan planning and advisory board made up of laymen and clergy—*The Michigan Catholic,* Feb. 1, March 17, March 31, 1966.

Vatican II treated the problems of today's dioceses with both objectivity and initiative. The repeated conciliar emphasis on the proper role of the laity in their dioceses was not confined to idealistic exhortation. Instead various types of conferences, commissions and pastoral councils involving both the laity and the lower clergy were specifically recommended as the expected pattern to be followed in achieving a wider dispersal of responsibility within dioceses. The *Constitution on the Church* referred to organs of communication as if they were already in existence.

> They [the laity] are, by reason of the knowledge, competence or outstanding ability which they may enjoy, permitted and sometimes even obliged to express their opinion on those things which concern the good of the Church. When occasions arise, let this be done through the organs erected by the Church for this purpose (CC 37).

But subsequent documents frankly indicated that the means for dialogue and shared responsibility would have to be either constructed or reorganized.

> Among the collaborators of the bishop in the government of the diocese are numbered those presbyters who constitute his senate, or council, such as the cathedral chapter, the board of consultors or other committees according to the circumstances or nature of various localities. These institutions, especially the cathedral chapters, should be reorganized wherever necessary in keeping with present day needs (DCP 27).

The *Decree on Priestly Life* made explicit what the other documents implicitly indicated: that a pastoral council should be representatively selected.

> They [the bishops] should gladly listen to their priests, indeed consult them and engage in dialogue with them in those matters which concern the necessities of pastoral work and welfare of the diocese. In order to put this into effect, there should be—in a manner suited to today's con-

ditions and necessities, and with a structure and norms to
be determined by law—a body or senate of priests representing all the priests. This representative body by its advice
will be able to give the bishop effective assistance in the
administration of the diocese (DPL 7).

The inclusion of a representative number of the laity in the
decision-making apparatus of the diocese is explicity cited in
the *Decree Concerning the Pastoral Office of Bishops.*

It is greatly desired that in each diocese a pastoral commission will be established over which the diocesan bishop
himself will preside and in which specially chosen clergy,
religious and lay people will participate. The duty of this
commission will be to investigate and weigh pastoral under-
takings and to formulate practical conclusions regarding
them (DCP 27).

It is important that these recommendations be seen in context. In those dioceses where prior to Vatican II there were no
councils or commissions assisting the bishop and where the
general de-Christianization of the area had statistically lowered
the possibility of large-scale involvement of the faithful in the
decision-making process of the Church, the creation of a particular commission or a pastoral council now represents a healthy
advance. But in those dioceses, particularly in the United States,
where non-representative and non-initiative displaying commissions and councils have been in existence for years without really
fulfilling the purpose announced by the council it will be necessary to improve the selection pattern and to expand the membership in order to achieve the goal of the council.

In the United States the logical implementation of the conciliar goal of shared responsibility within a diocese would seem
to involve some form of diocesan assembly representative of the
entire diocese. A diocesan assembly of representatives of all the
faithful would not be original either in the United States or in
the universal Church; when Bishop England developed one

form of assembly over one hundred fifty years ago he was returning to the frequent practice of the early Church, which was to consult the faithful within a given area to determine matters of consequence.

5. ASSEMBLY PROCEDURES

It is obvious that a considerable amount of advance preparation would be necessary to insure the success of a diocesan assembly. As in any representative body the delegates would be bearers of the views and the wisdom of those whom they represented. A diocesan assembly would require previous parish assemblies (similar to those discussed in the following chapter) by which the delegates could be elected and from which they would bring the expressed charisms of the faithful.

The diocesan assembly could follow the procedural pattern adopted by the Vatican Council itself.[9] Special commissions elected by the entire membership would prepare reports on current situations and prepare outlines of future projects.[10] These proposals would then be presented to the assembly and either accepted or returned to the respective commissions for modification. The results of pastoral research and experimenta-

9. The diocesan synod of Manchester, New Hampshire, includes 85 laity, 54 religious and 177 diocesan priests. Its commissions parallel those of Vatican II, e.g., the bishop and the government of the diocese; the pastoral formation of the clergy and the faithful; studies and seminaries; missions; liturgy; press and information media; Christian unity. The purpose of the synod, according to Bishop Ernest J. Primeau, will be "to renew the laws and regulations of the diocese in the tone and spirit of the council, and in conformity with the present legislation of the Catholic Church for the pastoral good of the People of God and the salvation of their souls."

10. Bishop Primeau has established a diocesan pastoral commission of priests, religious and laymen "to examine and weigh pastoral matters and to formulate practical conclusions regarding them." Membership of the commission includes 14 diocesan priests—10 of them elected by diocesan clergy and four appointed by the bishop. There are also five members representing religious communities of men, 10 members from women's religious communities, and 35 laymen chosen by the bishop on the advice of diocesan clergy.

tion could be reported to the assembly and future policy would be determined on its basis. The assembly could also authorize the additional research projects so necessary for future determination of possible commitments of resources.

There would also be the opportunity to devise patterns of mutual assistance among certain parishes. Some aspects of the problems of today's inner-city parishes are obviously beyond the isolated power of any one parish. Yet these same problems would be analyzed most efficiently if initial discussion were confined to those actually engaged in these parishes. In special conferences within the framework of the assembly representatives from inner-city parishes could collectively review their resources and possibilities. The situation would then be presented to the entire assembly for its collective deliberation and assistance. In their turn other parish conferences could bring their special problems and needs to the attention of all, thus stimulating a sense of common concern and mutual assistance *prior* to the adoption of specific directives.

The necessity of developing a sense of concern and a desire to help before issuing directives deserves special attention. A policy determined solely by authority without some form of open exchange of alternatives frequently fails to achieve its purpose because it is not adjusted to the full complexity of a problem which it did not completely review. And even in those rare instances when a non-consultative decision represents the best course of action it often fails to achieve its purpose because in its execution it receives only minimal energy from those who are simply directed to fulfill it.

The joint consideration of policy prior to decision brings planners and executors together for the reciprocal development of techniques and possibilities which would otherwise be ignored. It is important to recall that unity and harmonious cooperation among bishops was intensified because of the discussion and collective-decision policy followed in the open assembly of Vatican II. Thus a diocesan assembly could be expected not only to make clear to the entire people of God their responsibility for the problems and apostolates of all the members—a sizeable achievement in itself—but it would also lead to unity and harmonious action among all. The cooperation and coordination of efforts which the bishops achieved in their assembly could be the expected developments of a diocesan assembly under the direction of the bishop, a possibility suggested by the council's recognition of the value of collective direction.

> Various forms of the apostolate should be encouraged, and in the whole diocese or in any particular areas of it the coordination and close connection of all apostolic works should be fostered under the direction of the bishop. Thus all undertakings and organizations, be they catechetical, missionary, charitable, social, familial, educational, or anything else pursuing a pastoral aim, should be directed toward harmonious action. Thus at the same time the unity of the diocese will also be made more evident (DCP 17).

The ferment and the exchange of ideas initiated in a diocesan assembly could be continued throughout the year by the various commissions whose members would be elected by the assembly, for example, the Liturgical Commission, the Ecumenical Commission, the Board of Education, the Social Action Commission, and so forth. The chairmen of these commissions could constitute an advisory board for the bishop, each commission being recognized as sufficiently competent to make major decisions which in their final form would be subject to ratification by the bishop.

It would seem advisable to elect clergy to the various commissions according to a fixed proportion similar to the twelve laity-five clergy formula originally used by Bishop England. This procedure would make it possible for clergy and laity collectively to elect the entire commission. Priests elected to posi-

tions by all the people of God would have both the status and
the confidence to offer that type of independent judgment which
an appointed cleric cannot always make in major matters without some fear of loss of office. Elections restricted to deciding
only the lay members of a particular commission would deprive
the Church of the powers of discernment of its people in the
determination of potential candidates for the episcopal office.
The fact that innovating tendencies are not predominant characteristics of the hierarchy may be due to the current situation
in which initiative-assuming priests have only a very limited role
within the areas of competence from which bishops are selected.

Emphasis should be placed on the importance of electing
both clergy and laity to diocesan boards by *all* the faithful
engaged in a particular apostolate. In regard to this it will be
extremely helpful to recall the policy adopted by the council
fathers in selecting the members of the commissions responsible
for revising the conciliar documents. On October 12, 1962, the
council fathers declared a recess in order to elect these members
rather than accept the appointments which were being offered
without an open review of their qualifications. The bishops'
insistence on the use of the elective process to determine membership in these all-important commissions was not intended as
a rebuke to those previously nominated to these positions. It was
rather a reflection of their belief that only representatives freely
selected by the entire membership can accurately present the
opinion and the wisdom of all. This decision was certainly crucial for the success of Vatican II; the commission members
elected by all the bishops brought to the revision of the conciliar
documents a perspective that resulted in their progressive nature.

It would seem reasonable to apply the same elective principle within the diocesan assembly. For example, the members
of the diocesan board of education or any other board should
feel obligated to express the charisms possessed by the faithful
rather than merely reflect the recognized wisdom of the prelate,

as those honored by ecclesiastical appointment are unconsciously inclined to do. The expected exchange of opposing opinions within a commission reflecting the varying beliefs of the faithful would probably introduce a certain tension where it is not customary, but the resulting decisions would be enriched by the views and insights of all. And the sunlight of an open review of decisions would be a health-producing factor through its channeling of criticism into a usable form.

> In order that they may fulfill their function, let it be recognized that all the faithful, whether clerics or laity, possess a lawful freedom of inquiry, freedom of thought and of expressing their mind with humility and fortitude in those matters on which they enjoy competence (PCC 62).

The office of bishop would be considerably enhanced by a structure permitting him to preside and to determine on a fully informed basis. As teacher and leader the bishop would be in a position to direct the diocese after listening to and drawing upon the experience of a wide spectrum of individuals, namely, the parish faithful, the apostolic organizers, and the various experts.

6. ELECTION VS. SELECTION

In many dioceses it is becoming increasingly difficult for a bishop to exercise the necessary discernment in selecting the most suitable candidate for an office requiring a combination of abilities and talents. Most bishops would presumably appreciate a system which took advantage of the discerning power of many in analyzing competence and which removed from themselves any suspicion of favoritism or over-extended reliance on a small corps of inner advisors. If an elective process were followed it would no longer be necessary for the bishop to rely on the discernment powers of an already established group of advisors in selecting new candidates for executive positions within a diocese. The faithful actively engaged in a particular apostolate or commitment could collectively exercise far greater power of discernment in selecting executive coordinators of their actions, thus providing the bishop with a staff of proven competency and recognized rapport with the faithful—an ideal tool to assist him in his directive function.[11]

Each commission (Ecumenism, Education, Liturgy, and the rest) could be expected to serve as a clearing house through which the collective wisdom of all would be made available by a channeling of judgments and suggestions into a common source. A complete picture of the actual status of a particular apostolate could be presented objectively by those most familiar with the situation. Thus a psychological boost would be given to that great number of interested and articulate clergy and laity eager to serve the Church by providing them with an effective means of presenting their views and suggestions. It would appear inevitable that a faster implementation of decisions would result from a collective sharing in the presentation of information and opinion prior to decision.

Of course provision would have to be made for the non-elected, non-solicited contribution. The various commissions would be expected to hold open meetings at regular intervals in which any number of the people of God could offer a report or an opinion which he regarded as necessary for consideration. The Council's *Declaration on Religious Freedom* refers to the fact that a sense of duty will prompt individuals to arrive at independent judgment regarding various matters.

> The demand is increasingly made that men should act on their own judgment, enjoying and making use of a responsible freedom, not driven by coercion but motivated by a sense of duty (DRF 1).

It will be therefore incumbent upon the Church to provide

11. When Archbishop Martin M. Johnson of Vancouver submitted to a diocesan-wide vote his proposal for putting control of the diocesan schools in the hands of elected laymen, he received a remarkable 90% approval from his people—*National Catholic Reporter,* June, 1965.

some mechanism by which the voice of individual dissent can be given a hearing within its official structure.

Each commission would also adopt the policy of regularly consulting individuals of recognized competence within their field, a practice which would be particularly beneficial in the matter of planning future diocesan projects.[12] A Diocesan Planning Commission would obviously require the consultation service of urban experts to assess adequately the future needs of the Church in a given area and to establish research machinery for determining future policy.

> The forms of the apostolate should be properly adapted to the needs of the present day with regard not only for man's spiritual and moral circumstances but also for his social, demographic, and economic conditions. Religious and social research, through offices of pastoral sociology, contributes much to the efficacious and fruitful attainment of that goal, and it is highly recommended (DCP 17).

Should the Church begin to build chapels in high-rise apartments? Should the Church choose to establish trade schools in the inner-city rather than continue to maintain parochial and secondary schools? And would the Church be best served in the future by replacing inner-city rectories with "team institutes" utilizing a combination of clergy and laity? Only research and experimentation will provide reasonably adequate answers to questions which can best be answered by preparing possible solutions in advance. To wait until conditions reach a point where only a limited number of alternatives are possible is to betray the vast resources of personnel and finance contributed to the Church with the understanding that they be used with wisdom.

12. The Archdiocese of Baltimore has received a series of reports on what urban developments can be expected in that area during the next twenty years from Father Robert G. Howes, a priest with a degree in City and Regional Planning from the Massachusetts Institute of Technology—*National Catholic Reporter,* January 19, 1966.

A representative restructuring of dioceses along lines permitting maximum participation and communication among all the faithful will require considerable effort and energy from all involved, hierarchy, clergy and laity. But do we have a choice? In the *Constitution on the Church* the Holy Spirit has spoken to us of the "wonderful things" which may be expected from a "familiar dialogue" between clergy and laity:

> In the laity a strengthened sense of personal responsibility, a renewed enthusiasm, a more ready application of their talents . . . the latter, on the other hand, aided by the experience of the laity can more clearly and decisively come to decisions regarding both spiritual and temporal matters. In this way the whole church strengthened by each one of its members may more effectively fulfill its mission for the life of the world.

Can we really expect that the constitution's ideal of close communication and collaboration between clergy and laity will operate without formal structures? It would seem reasonable to predict that the *Constitution on the Church,* with its vision of the people of God as a communal body perfecting itself by charismatic exchanges among all its members, will not become a reality until such time as the faithful by an elective process can bestow specific mandates to communicate upon those most qualified to reflect the collective wisdom of all.

> The laity derive the right and duty to the apostolate from their union with Christ the head; incorporated into Christ's Mystical Body through Baptism and strengthened by the power of the Holy Spirit through Confirmation, they are assigned to the apostolate by the Lord Himself. . . . For the exercise of this apostolate, the Holy Spirit who sanctifies the people of God through ministry and the sacraments gives the faithful special gifts also "allotting them to everyone according as He wills" . . . From the acceptance of these charisms, including those which are more elementary, there arise for each believer the right and duty to use them

in the Church and in the world for the good of men and the building up of the Church, in the freedom of the Holy Spirit who "breathes where He wills" (DOL 3).

It would seem unrealistic to expect that the Church can have the benefit of gifts of the Spirit "allotting them to everyone according as He wills" unless we are prepared to establish a system of open assembly where the gifts can be presented. Past experience should make it fairly obvious by now that there is going to be no representative communication (how indicative of public opinion are a few letters to the bishop, or individual confrontations with the pastor?) unless structures are created which facilitate true dialogue among *all* the faithful. Not to create the necessary structures is in effect to impede Vatican II.

In the process of restructuring, the experience of the American representative process is a singular gift to the Church. In the United States there is a long tradition of participation by the people in the life of the community and a sense of shared responsibility for the good of all. A balance of responsibility, authority and freedom of initiative has been achieved which could be extremely beneficial if adopted in Church life.

It is important to recall that the Church has made many such adaptations in the past: to the imperial court system of Constantine, for example, and to the feudal structure of medieval Europe. The adaptation to the representative system now prevalent would be in keeping with the tendencies of shared authority in the Church from the very beginning, tendencies which were retained even during periods of strict authoritarianism in the heavily influential temporal order. In fact the adaptation to the representative system would probably have occurred earlier if the Church had not been forced into a defensive position by reformation and enlightenment. In this regard the American Church may have established a helpful precedent. Over a century ago Pope Gregory XVI indicated that Bishop John England had acted in keeping with the Church's historical policy of adapting the human aspects of its structure to its environment while, at the same time, preserving the divinely constituted element.

One of the reforms seriously considered at Vatican II was the advisability of electing the pope for a single ten-year term. Further consideration of this proposal would obviously have implications regarding a similar term for every bishop. For example, would it be desirable to elect bishops by the assembly of each diocese for an eight-year non-renewable term? The most distinguished of the nation's prelates would undoubtedly be elected again at a later date in some other diocese. The wide experience of bishops honored by a second or third election would benefit every diocese over which they presided. Instead of the current practice of dividing an over-sized diocese only on the occasion of the bishop's death, the splitting of a diocese into more manageable units could occur at the end of an eight-year term, wherever necessary. The present auxiliary bishops could be expected to become bishops in the new and smaller jurisdictions, a function more in keeping with their role than the prevalent practice of using them as confirmation specialists or episcopal stand-ins.[13]

The election of bishops for a fixed term would end the difficult problem of securing the retirement of an individual bishop when necessary, as the decision to elect or not to elect a particular individual bishop with an outstanding record could be made on the basis of the competence he still displayed.[14] The general practice of electing bishops for a fixed term could pre-

13. For a discussion of the role of auxiliary bishops in the church, see Karl Rahner, S.J., *Bishops: Their Status and Function* (Baltimore: Helicon, 1964), pp. 27 ff.

14. Forty-five archbishops and bishops, or almost one-third of the acting heads of U. S. dioceses, are 70 or older, according to the reports of a survey appearing in the *National Catholic Reporter*, July 14, 1965.

sent the opportunity to implement effectively what is regarded as one of the most difficult recommendations of Vatican II.

> Since the pastoral office of bishops is so important and weighty, diocesan bishops and others regarded in law as their equals, who have become less capable of fulfilling their duties properly because of the increasing burden of age or some other serious reason, are earnestly requested to offer their resignation from office either at their own initiative or upon the invitation of the competent authority. If the competent authority should accept the resignation, it will make provision both for the suitable support of those who have resigned and for special rights to be accorded them (DCP 21).

A fringe benefit of the elective system would be the resulting rotation in office of appointive episcopal aides; each new bishop would probably be inclined to reassess the individual talents under his jurisdiction.

An elective pattern would recognize the exhausting process of public life—a lifetime of ecclesiastical tenure can actually shorten a life span by its unending demands. It would also provide the Church with the benefits of new insights and a periodic appraisal of efforts through a regular turnover of the presiding official.

Eight years would not seem to be too short a term of office since under the present system the most talented bishops frequently spend far shorter periods in various dioceses during their rise to greater responsibilities. An eight-year term would actually stabilize tenure in certain cases, by requiring a full term before election to a larger diocese. It would also permit a wider flexibility in selecting and evaluating episcopal leadership throughout the entire nation.

The regular relinquishment of the office of authority would clearly indicate that authority is held in the Church as a *service* accompanied by the humility and simplicity of life resulting from a clear realization that he who goes up will eventually come down.

> They should also be mindful of their obligation to give an example of holiness in charity, humility, and simplicity of life. . . . In exercising their office of father and pastor, bishops should stand in the midst of their people as those who serve (DCP 15 - 16).

The collegiate nature of shared responsibility within the Church would be obvious through again accepting the voice of the faithful as an expression of the spirit in the selective process.[15] Smaller bishoprics could conceivably be created as shared authority within larger areas becomes the accepted norm among the bishops of the area.

> They [the bishops] exercise this office individually in reference to the portions of the Lord's flock assigned to them, each one taking care of the particular church committed to him, or sometimes some of them jointly providing for certain common needs of various churches (DCP 3).

As a result each individual bishop would be in closer contact with its faithful and more clearly seen as the father of the flock.[16]

> Let them be good shepherds who know their sheep and whose sheep know them. Let them be true fathers who excel in the spirit of love and solicitude for all and to whose divinely conferred authority all gratefully submit themselves. Let them so gather and mold the whole family of their flock that everyone, conscious of his own duties, may live and work in the communion of love.
>
> In order effectively to accomplish these things, bishops, "ready for every good work" (2 Tim 2:21) and "enduring

---

15. Cf. Acts 6:1-3. St. Leo's formula in Epistle 10.4 (*Qui Praefuturus Est Omnibus, Ab Omnibus Eligatur*) and the formula of Celestine I in Epistle 4, 6.5 (*Nullus Invitis Detur Episcopus*) date from the councils and popes of the fourth and fifth centuries.

16. For an analysis of the theological significance of a diocese, see Rahner, *op. cit.*, pp. 34 ff.

all things for the sake of the chosen ones" (3 Tim 2:10),
should arrange their life in such a way as to accommodate
it to the needs of our times (DCP 16).

There would also be the possibility of electing younger bishops
when a potential thirty- or forty-year reign in office would not
be an inhibiting factor to the electors. There is not much point
in citing the intricacies of diocesan management as justifying a
lengthy term in office in order to permit the bishop to achieve a
familiarity with his diocese. A restructuring of dioceses along
lines of shared responsibility, together with the division of the
larger dioceses into more manageable units, would enable each
bishop to exercise his office in the spirit of Vatican II. An eight-
year term would offer sufficient opportunity for a reasonably
competent individual to fulfill the office with the energy and
decisiveness of one who knows that his office of service will be
terminated and his own stewardship reviewed by the faithful.

The present method of electing bishops confines the voting
to a relatively small number of individuals. The official plan is
that the bishops in each province should annually send to Rome
the names of several priests whom they consider suitable candidates for the office of bishop.[17] The character and performance
of those recommended is determined by letter and sworn testimony from a number of individuals and their names are filed
with the Congregation of the Consistory which serves in an
advisory capacity to the pope in the naming of bishops. In practice the apostolic delegate and a small number of key bishops
determine every episcopal appointment in the United States
including the work-up policy by which bishops of proven competence and reliability are successively transferred from smaller
to larger dioceses.

Although the system has worked reasonably well in the past,
a proper interpretation of collegiality would seem to make it

17. Cf. "The Bishop," *The New Catholic Encyclopedia.*

necessary that the number of electors be expanded to include the entire hierarchy and at least a sampling of the clergy and the laity. A frank and open discussion of the present problems in selecting bishops would be most beneficial to the American Church. The majority of the clergy and an increasing number of the laity are familiar with the machinery of ecclesiastical promotion, and honesty in the Church will require an objective review of the means used to determine the will of the Spirit in the selection of bishops. With the number of bishops in the world rapidly approaching three thousand, there are few educated Catholics who will seriously regard references to papal selection as a legitimate explanation.

The inclusion of the people of God in the selection of bishops would be particularly appropriate now that the Church has officially excluded a far less reliable source of selection.

> This Sacred Ecumenical Synod declares that the right of nominating and appointing bishops belongs properly, peculiarly, and *per se* exclusively to the competent ecclesiastical authority.
> Therefore, for the purpose of duly protecting the freedom of the Church and of promoting more conveniently and efficiently the welfare of the faithful, this holy Council desires that in future no more rights or privileges of election, nomination, presentation, or designation for the office of bishop be granted to civil authorities. The civil authorities, on the other hand, whose favorable attitude toward the Church the sacred synod gratefully acknowledges and highly appreciates, are most kindly requested voluntarily to renounce the above-mentioned rights and privileges which they presently enjoy by reason of a treaty or custom, after discussing the matter with the Apostolic See (DCP 20).

There are various methods of electing that could be employed. An annual point system might be found preferable to a specific election every eight years; the diocesan assembly each year could secretly ballot on individuals inside or outside the diocese who would be considered as competent to serve as a future bishop. At the expiration of the eight-year term of the current bishop all the ballots during the eight years would be counted with the highest eligible candidate being nominated for final approval by the national hierarchy and by the Holy See. An episcopal election conducted by a diocesan assembly would understandably involve a certain amount of politics. But we have politics under the present system as well; no one is ever made a bishop without the approval of several key officials who are convinced of his ability.[18]

> With the help of the Holy Spirit, it is the task of the entire People of God, especially pastors and theologians, to hear, distinguish and interpret the many voices of our age, and to judge them in the light of the divine Word, so that revealed truth can always be more deeply penetrated, better understood and set forth to greater advantage (PCC 44).

Would it not seem appropriate that the similar problem of selecting leaders to execute this function also be presented to the discerning wisdom of the people of God? The election of Church leaders was not originally a clerical preserve, and there is very good evidence that it need not be. America's first Catholic bishop, John Carroll, was nominated by his clergy. The great religious orders have historically relied on the elective process to select leaders.

The restructuring of the Church may appear to be a radical departure to those who regard as indispensable the structuring

18. Father John J. Wordeman has suggested that in the election of bishops, a) each secular priest would have one vote; b) each religious congregation or order of men and women active in the diocese would have one vote; c) each parish would elect two voting delegates, men or women; d) one vote would be cast by a delegate of each diocesan organization, e.g., the St. Vincent de Paul Society, the Legion of Mary; e) the election would be held at an electoral assembly much like that held in the Sistine Chapel for the election of the Bishop of Rome—*National Catholic Reporter,* April, 1966.

which the Church acquired during the Middle Ages. Others may feel that the hierarchical nature of the Church does not permit a democratic structuring. In actuality a new structure could be regarded as a return to an earlier and more life-giving form. Cyprian's personal rule[19] that he would make no episcopal decision without consulting priests, deacons and people, has been imitated by those most successful in ecclesiastical organizations (for example, St. Benedict), and at this late date there are few who would question the wisdom of the laity who elected an Ambrose and an Augustine to episcopal sees.[20]

The *Constitution on the Church* with its vision of the Church as uniquely communal and the Council's recognition of the multiple charisms of the faithful offer a definite challenge of implementation to the American Church. Nowhere else in the world is there at the disposal of the Mystical Body so great a talent and natural inclination to develop the organizational structures necessary to make the vision a reality.[21]

19. "I have made it a rule, ever since the beginning of my episcopate, to make no decision merely on the strength of my own personal opinion without consulting you (the priests and the deacons), without the approbation of the people"—St. Cyprian, Epist. 14.4.
20. "The rules for election to the episcopate in the early Church are well known in their broad lines from the correspondence of St. Cyprian (d. 258), and from the Canons of Hippolytus and the Apostolic Constitutions, documents not so securely dated but here reflecting early third-century tradition. The elements guaranteeing valid episcopal institution are enumerated by Cyprian thus: judgment of God, good recommendation by the clergy, suffrage of the people, consent of other bishops. . . . It was a matter of ensuring the promotion of the *most suitable* person; so the faithful, who were well acquainted with each one's merits, had to add their opinion to that of the clergy"—Congar, *op. cit.*, p. 232.
21. "In every diocese . . . there are laymen of exceptional competence in many fields . . . They know instinctively that the Church offers them a meaningful challenge. . . . they must be respected and consulted within the limits of the tasks they are asked to accomplish; they must get the feeling that their work is important; they must be given recognition"—Episcopal Committee, "Interim Report on the Greater Participation and Involvement of the Laity in the Life and Work of the Church," Nov., 1965.

Chapter Two

THE CHURCH AT THE GRASS ROOTS: THE PARISH—STRUCTURES AND PERSONNEL

"He was the parish priest of the world."

John XXIII would probably have appreciated that compliment made by a close friend shortly after the pope's death. Although other Church institutions and their personnel often draw more attention, the parish in which priest and people share the Christian life continues to be regarded as an ideal structure in the process of making Christ present in the world. At the Canadian Social Week in 1953 the then Monsignor Montini stated the case for the parish: "the parish, the cell closest to man and therefore the best adapted to form the personal, familial, and community life is for these reasons the most indispensable to society." The success or failure of Vatican II may ultimately depend on what Chistians do in the community they are accustomed to call the parish.

But what should a parish be? In its present form, is it a permanent element in the Church? Or should today's parish be modified—or even radically restructured? The answer we now give to this question will have an immense effect on the future life of the Church.

It is important to recall that today's territorial parish with its neat, clearly defined geographical borders and its Christian commitment concentrated in that area is a development of the

Middle Ages. In the early centuries the Church in urban areas adopted a radial or "team" form of penetration in which the bishop, clergy and elders formed one association jointly responsible for the Christianization of an entire city. Only in the eleventh century under the influence of feudalism did the Church begin to adopt the division of urban areas into jurisdictional units similar to today's parishes.[1]

Even when it became a geographical division the parish initially retained elements of its former pattern of shared responsibility between clergy and laity. In many medieval parishes it was the custom that each adult have a vote in the management of the parish and its activities. The representatives of the people in parochial work were the Church wardens, who were chosen by vote at annual parish meetings. Their duties included the care of Church finances and buildings as well as the management of Church property.[2]

This tradition of clergy-lay association in the direction of parish life did not endure after the Reformation. The breakdown of the Church's organizational control at that time provoked compensatory action in which the shared authority pattern of earlier ages was seriously curtailed by ecclesiastical authority. As a result of the Council of Trent a disciplined clergy with direct control over all phases of Church activity became the accepted norm. Strictly clerical control of parish life was emphasized by Church law and custom, without establishing or even recognizing the earlier structure of lay involvement.[3]

The United States inherited this Tridentine pattern of parish

1. The concept of parish (Greek *paroikia*, Latin *paroecia*) has developed through the centuries; originally referring to the people and their community, it is now generally accepted as referring to a designated territory. For an account of the historical development of the parish, see Alex Blochlinger, *The Modern Parish Community* (New York: Kenedy, 1965).

2. Cf. Gasquet, *Parish Life in Medieval England.*

3. Cf. Blochlinger, *op. cit.*, pp. 92 ff.

life with its concentration of Christian energy within a determined area and its habit of exclusively clerical management. But
it is significant that from its very beginning the American parish
enjoyed more success than its European counterpart. The increasing alienation between clergy and faithful and the subsequent
de-Christianization of large areas of Europe in the nineteenth
century did not occur in the United States. Many factors contributed to the phenomenon of a vast growth of the Church in
the United States at a time when world Catholicism was generally in a state of decline. Certainly the financial neutrality of
the American government toward religious bodies and their
institutions could be regarded as one of the more important factors in the establishment of successful parish life. Unlike its
European counterpart the American parish united clergy and
faithful in a building program and financial partnership of staggering dimensions. The united energy expended in construction
efforts and the collective pride resulting from the creation of
impressive structures produced a feeling of common involvement in the life of the Church which was not found in areas
where it had long been established. Even excessive cases of
clerical dominance were accepted as a tolerable element in
obtaining success in common efforts.

Today's parish is obviously in a transitional stage. The
environment and the mentality of its earlier period of development are rapidly changing. In many areas the immense building
projects of the past are continued, but the circumstances and the
contributing personnel are different. There is a general feeling
of uncertainty as the patterns of the past seem increasingly less
applicable, while new forms of parish life requiring imagination
and initiative are difficult to introduce into the inherited pattern.

The inherited pattern of parish life in the United States
appears in many forms. There is the inner-city, Gothic giant of
the immigrant period, now surrounded by tenements and housing projects. There are the new, estate-like suburban parishes

with their sculptured lawns and building complexes. There is the small town parish with its architecture reminiscent of an earlier America. And there is the rural parish with its satellite "mission" chapels drawing the faithful from their distant homes.

But although the forms vary the basic problem remains the same. How does the Church, a supernatural reality, effectively incarnate itself in some form of local structure and pattern of activity so that God's saving act can be made present among men here and now?[4]

It is a difficult problem in any age. In our own it becomes extremely difficult due to the growing complexity of the situation in which the Christian life must become incarnate. The population shift from towns to the great urban centers, the high mobility rate of the average American family, the phenomenon of the high-rise apartment with its transient clientele, and other dis-associative elements within American society are drastically reducing the opportunity of forming Christian communities with the required sense of continuity among the membership.[5] The enormous population growth of the Church within the United States combined with the necessity of establishing parishes sufficiently large to finance collectively the debts involved in huge building projects have produced a tendency to form larger parishes. As a result the possibility of developing meaningful contacts between clergy and parishioner and between parishioner and parishioner is substantially lowered.

The maintaining of personal encounters among the faithful was a basic accomplishment of parishes of an earlier era. Its

4. "Despite its universal destiny and its relation to all men, the Church is essentially destined to be localized . . . ; the Church itself only becomes most wholly and intensively event in the local celebration of the Eucharist" —Hugo Rahner, *The Parish* (Westminster: Newman, 1958), p. 32.

5. "From New York, Chicago, San Francisco to Tokyo, Manila, Bombay, in Africa and Latin America, priests told me that constant moving causes the traditional census to become obsolete even before it is completed"—Bernard F. Meyer, M.M., *The Whole World is My Neighbor* (Notre Dame, Ind.: Fides, 1964), p. 29.

continuance is of crucial importance if the parish is to project the redemptive work of Christ on the person to person basis which has characterized Christianity during its periods of most successful impact upon society. The problem is intensified by the fact that techniques used with some success in the past now seem to be losing their effectiveness. Parish organizations which once offered vital lines of communication among the faithful are now generally considered as involving only ten percent of those attending Church in a particular area. Their original ability to coordinate apostolic commitments and to reflect a parish consensus has been comprised by the fact that for various reasons they no longer attract a representative segment of the parish membership.[6] Nor does it appear likely that the organizations of the past have a format of operation capable of being transferred to situations radically different from the environment in which the organizations were established. For example, the suburban migration of the middle class has produced an inner-city parish with its own distinctive problems which have been found impervious to the traditional methods of organization.[7] And to add a note of urgency to the over-all situation there is some evidence that the once solid bond between clergy and laity within parishes is beginning to be weakened as an educated laity start to question the management decisions and ecclesiastical techniques of the clergy and—more importantly—the over-all direction of the apostolic efforts within parishes.[8]

6. "It is my observation that today organizational effort is not attractive to many of our Catholic men. There is no question that these men are willing to serve the proper needs of the church by a reasonable use of their talents, time and energy. They are too busy, however, with their business, social, and family life to obligate themselves to a routine of meetings, projects, and time-consuming programs which in their judgment are too far removed from the urgent needs of modern times"—Bishop John King Mussio of Steubenville, Ohio, in a pastoral letter.

7. For a Protestant view of the current crisis in parish life, see the booklet published by the National Council of Churches in 1963, *Where in the World*, and its sequel, *What in the World*.

8. "It would be a disservice to the church to deny the presence in our

Under the influence of Vatican II many United States parishes are in the process of evolving into forms capable of responding to the changing needs of the American Church. But before considering the forms that the life of the faithful is assuming in these parishes it may be helpful to recall the type of parish structure predominant in certain areas of the United States a decade ago.

1. THE PARISH AND THE COUNCIL

In the decade before Vatican II the traditional pattern in the United States parish was that a pastor and one or more assistant pastors would share a common residence known as a rectory, which was usually located near the parish church. The pastor was selected by the bishop of the diocese, generally on the basis of seniority, and was in complete control of parish life. He made all the major decisions regarding the spiritual and financial status of the parish. He interpreted the mind of the bishop, determined the needs of the parish, established the pattern of worship, supervised educational efforts, controlled parish organizations and was the single point of authority and responsibility within the parish. Varying amounts of influence were brought to bear on his decisions by the assistant pastors, certain predominant parishioners and those parishioners who might write to the bishop if displeased. But in practice most pastors could be as authoritative or as permissive as they chose, depending on their personality and the endorsement or tolerance of the bishop of the diocese.

The assistant pastors were also selected by the bishop for their particular assignment and were usually younger priests who would serve in one or more parishes before becoming pastors. They were under the direct supervision of the pastor who

---

midst of symptoms that suggest an anti-clerical sentiment hitherto unknown to American Catholics"—Monsignor John Tracy Ellis, "The Catholic Layman in America Today," *Commonweal*, June 22, 1962.

would assign various functions to them, for example, the direction of particular organizations such as the Holy Name Society and the Sodality. In order to be official their decisions needed the endorsement of the pastor, although in practice many pastors permitted a fair degree of autonomy with the understanding that all major decisions would be referred to them for final approval.

In those parishes with a parochial school the sisters devoted their efforts to the education of the young. The actual percentage of Catholic children living within the parish who were being educated by the sisters varied greatly; each year it was becoming evident that a declining percentage of the parish children were attending the parochial school. The sisters generally restricted their apostolate to the school and only occasionally did they affect parish life apart from their program within the school.[9]

The faithful living within the geographical confines of the parish were generally referred to as the laity. Their apostolic activity was usually limited to programs within the parish, although through financial contributions their support reached other areas. From the parish the laity received the word of God and the sacraments of the Church; in turn they offered various forms of assistance to the parish. That assistance could be financial (expected from all), participation in parish organizations (limited by circumstances to a minority), or advice and consultation (from only a few).

Would these generalizations regarding certain parishes of a decade ago be applicable today? In some areas they would seem to apply; in others they would not.[10] But the more impor-

9. Cf. Daniel Callahan, ed., *Generation of the Third Eye* (New York: Sheed and Ward, 1965). For most of the 22 contributors to this symposium of viewpoints of the young Catholics the parish was not a formative influence.

10. For an attempt to examine the attitudes of clergy and laity in the American church, see Joseph H. Fichter, *Priest and People* (New York:

tant question is to determine whether this type of parish is what the Holy Spirit expects of us in the new era of Vatican II. Should a parish structure corresponding to the above description be permitted to continue in existence or should it be substantially modified in the light of Vatican II?[11] The *Constitution on the Church* would seem to indicate a radically different type of relationship among clergy and laity from that which characterized parish life in certain areas before the council and which may still be prevalent in some localities today.

> For the nurturing and constant growth of the People of God, Christ the Lord instituted in His Church a variety of ministries, which work for the good of the whole body. For those ministers, who are endowed with sacred power, serve their brethren, so that all who are of the People of God, and therefore enjoy a true Christian dignity, working toward a common goal freely and in an orderly way, may arrive at salvation (CC 18).

> Pastors know how much the laity contribute to the welfare of the entire Church. They also know that they were not ordained by Christ to take upon themselves alone the entire salvific mission of the Church toward the world. On the contrary they understand that it is their noble duty to shepherd the faithful and to recognize their ministries and charisms, so that all according to their proper roles may cooperate in this common undertaking with one mind. . . . These faithful are by baptism made one body with Christ and are constituted among the People of God; they are in their own way made sharers in the priestly, prophetical, and kingly functions of Christ; and they carry out for their own part the mission of the whole Christian people in the Church and in the world (CC 30 - 31).

Sheed and Ward, 1965). Father Fichter's study is based on questionnaires and interviews of over 2,000 parish priests and over 2,000 lay Catholics.

11. "Today's parish is hopelessly outdated. Patchwork reform is useless. The parish must be struck by the revolution that is sweeping the church; it must be completely, radically restructured"—Bishop Mussio of Steubenville in *Ave Maria*, March 7, 1964.

Now the laity are called in a special way to make the
Church present and operative in those places and circumstances where only through them can it become the salt of
the earth. . . . Upon all the laity, therefore, rests the noble
duty of working to extend the divine plan of salvation to
all men of each epoch and in every land. Consequently,
may every opportunity be given them so that, according to
their abilities and the needs of the times, they may zealously
participate in the saving work of the Church (CC 33).

It is not only through the sacraments and the ministries of
the Church that the Holy Spirit sanctifies and leads the
people of God and enriches it with virtues, but, "allotting
his gifts to everyone according as He wills," He distributes
special graces among the faithful of every rank. . . . These
charisms, whether they be the more outstanding or the
more simple and widely diffused, are to be received with
thanksgiving and consolation for they are perfectly suited
to and useful for the needs of the Church (CC 12).

They [the laity] are, by reason of the knowledge, competence or outstanding ability which they may enjoy, permitted and sometimes even obliged to express their opinion
on those things which concern the good of the Church.
When occasions arise, let this be done through the organs
erected by the Church for this purpose. . . .
    Let the spiritual shepherds recognize and promote the
dignity as well as the responsibility of the laity in the
Church. Let them willingly employ their prudent advice.
Let them confidently assign duties to them in the service
of the Church, allowing them freedom and room for action.
Further, let them encourage lay people so that they may
undertake tasks on their own initiative (CC 37).

A great many wonderful things are to be hoped for from
this familiar dialogue between the laity and their spiritual
leaders: in the laity a strengthened sense of personal responsibility; a renewed enthusiasm; a more ready application of
their talents to the projects of their spiritual leaders. The
latter, on the other hand, aided by the experience of the
laity, can more clearly and more incisively come to decisions

regarding both spiritual and temporal matters. In this way, the whole Church, strengthened by each one of its members, may more effectively fulfill its mission for the life of the world (CC 37).

It is significant that in the *Constitution on the Church* the fathers of Vatican II preferred to consider Christian life not in the juridical concepts of parishes considered as institutions but rather in personal terms of what individual Christians could do under the influence of grace *in the execution of their own distinctive ministry*. The Constitution's approach to Christian life within the parish is apparently modeled on St. Paul's recognition of the roles given to the various members of each Christian community.

> Now there are varieties of gifts, but the same Spirit; and there are varieties of ministries, but the same Lord; and there are varieties of workings, but the same God, who works all things in all. Now the manifestation of the Spirit is given to everyone for profit. To one through the Spirit is given the utterance of wisdom; and to another the utterance of knowledge, according to the same Spirit; to another faith, in the same Spirit; to another the gift of healing, in the one Spirit; to another the working of miracles; to another prophecy; to another the distinguishing of spirits; to another various kinds of tongues; to another interpretation of tongues. But all these things are the work of one and the same Spirit, who divides to everyone according as he will (1 Cor 12:4-11).

What can our parishes do to achieve the ideal of parish life desired by the Spirit speaking through Vatican II? The council's proposals as presented in its various documents are necessarily general, and require both reflection and experimentation to determine satisfactory methods of realization within the daily life of parishes. But on the basis of published accounts of various attempts at implementing the conciliar documents in different parishes it is possible to present a composite picture of the direction of current efforts and a reasonable projection of subsequent developments.[12]

2. THE BLUEPRINT STAGE

The procedure of parish renewal as intended by Vatican II requires an initial expenditure of effort by all the faithful, clergy, sisters and laity, in a carefully executed program of study regarding both the actual condition of their parish and the decrees of the council. Both elements should receive attention—an objective analysis of the existing pattern of parish life and a thoughtful reflection on the application of the council documents to daily life within the parish—if the desired renewal is to be achieved according to the spirit of Vatican II. The process would require several months of intensive effort in both parish meetings and in home discussions. The *Constitution on the Church,* the theme document of the council, could be presented as the first topic for collective examination while the other documents would be studied and discussed in turn.

3. AT THE LAUNCHING PAD

The second phase of parish renewal generally involves some form of assembly in which all parishioners meet to present collectively plans and suggestions for an improved pattern of parish life on the basis of their reflection on the decrees of the council. The essential element at this point is to provide the opportunity for every member of the parish to present his particular insight into the life of the parish in a forum where it can be examined and evaluated.[13] On the basis of a balanced consideration of the

12. For an analysis of present parish structures and future possibilities, see the collection of articles on "Reforming the Parish," *Commonweal,* March 25, 1966.

13. Fichter found that the single change most desired in parish life by the laity was their greater involvement in the parish and closer ties with the clergy—*Op. cit.,* p. 187.

views of all it will be possible to frame the possible directions
of reform prior to actual decisions.

> The laity should accustom themselves to working in the
> parish in union with their priests, bringing to the Church
> community their own and the world's problems as well as
> questions concerning human salvation, all of which they
> should examine and resolve by deliberating in common. As
> far as possible the laity ought to provide helpful collabo-
> ration for every apostolic and missionary undertaking spon-
> sored by their local parish (DOL 10).

4. THE COMPONENTS OF RENEWAL

The next phase may be initiated with the formation of a number of committees to involve and to coordinate the effort and
wisdom of the entire membership in the affairs of the parish.[14]
A list of possible committees would include the following:

A Renewal Committee. Its purpose would be to provide for
a continual renewal through the planning of study and discussion groups, guest speakers and some program of religious education reaching all age groups within the parish. Its members
would also analyze the means of spiritual formation currently
available to the layman and make recommendations to improve
its effectiveness.

---

14. Diocesan statutes in various dioceses (e.g., Pittsburgh) require the
establishment of lay parish committees with a definite responsibility in the
direction of parish affairs. The committees cited here are developed from
those proposed in the Archdiocese of St. Louis.

Under the nineteenth century system of lay trusteeism abuses occurred
due to faulty delineation of responsibility and improper incorporation of
property. It is significant that these are no longer being cited as dangers
to be considered in lay involvement in parish affairs. For an account of the
origin of lay trusteeism, see Peter Guilday, *The Life and Times of John
Carroll, Archbishop of Baltimore, 1735-1815* (New York, 1922), Vol. I, pp.
782 ff. See also, Daniel Callahan, *The Mind of the Catholic Layman* (New
York: Charles Scribner's Sons, 1963), pp. 17 ff. Callahan finds two or
three elements working together as responsible for individual cases of
abuse: a pliant or machiavellian priest and an ignorant or rebellious group
of trustees.

A Liturgical Committee. This committee would continually evaluate the parish worship. It would care for the choir, the ushers, lectors, commentators and servers, and provide for the general needs of the church building and its upkeep. It would also supervise the administrative details connected with the conferral of the sacraments, such as marriage and confirmation celebrations.

The Christian Justice Committee. The members of this group would coordinate the various charitable and social programs conducted by the different parish organizations, for example, the Holy Name Society, the Sodality, the Legion of Mary and the St. Vincent de Paul Society. These groups would retain their autonomous status but would collectively become related parts of a broad social and charitable enterprise within the parish.

The Financial Committee. This committee would assist the pastor in problems connected with the financial support of the parish. Its concerns would include the development of alternative parish support plans, for example, a tithing program replacing weekly collections,[15] the possibility of maintenance and repair services performed by parish volunteers, and so forth. It would also review expenditures and make recommendations regarding the most suitable use of parish funds, such as assistance to poorer parishes.

The Ecumenical Committee. Its purpose would be to foster mutually beneficial encounters in worship and in charitable activities with groups holding other beliefs. Through special studies its members would acquaint themselves with the wide range of ecumenical possibilities regarding both worship and service to the community in union with members of other or no

15. The Diocese of Belleville, Illinois, has officially adopted a new "Christian Renewal" stewardship program designed to increase lay participation in church programs. The program bans all fund-raising projects for church support in favor of tithing.

faiths. On the basis of its investigations the committee would propose special projects and make general recommendations designed to develop better relationships among the various Churches in the area.

The Youth Committee. The purpose of this committee would be to consider the special needs of the younger parishioners and to plan programs adapted to these needs. The committee would have a policy of cooperating with other religious and civic groups in providing a common youth program beneficial to the entire community.

The School Committee. This committee would meet regularly with the pastor and school principal and would serve as an advisory board in both the direction of the parish school and in the determination of its policies and needs. Through contact with the local school board, the committee would attempt to share insights and to develop extra-curricular educational programs beneficial to all the children of the community. One of its goals would be the maximum utilization of the school facility and its personnel by the entire community through programs of adult education, job training, and so on.

The Diocesan Committee. Members of this committee would serve as liaison personnel constantly acquiring a familiarity with programs being developed in other parishes. They would also be responsible for bringing state, urban and county programs to the attention of the parish.

How would members be selected for the various committees? In the initial stage it would seem advisable to adopt a policy of combining volunteer and pastor appointees, the latter being necessary to secure a balance of talent throughout the committees. Once the precise role of each committee had been experienced by parishioners it would be possible to initiate an elective procedure by which the entire parish could select personnel with a record of interest and ability in the various committees. Elected members would then serve as the key personnel in the various committees which would remain open to volunteers.

A number of committee positions could be determined on a geographical basis so that each section of the parish would have the benefit of a neighborhood consultant on the various parish programs. The establishment of definite terms of service and the selection of some form of liturgical recognition to clearly indicate that committee service represented a unique gift to Christ in the parish would help to overcome the understandable hesitancy of many of the faithful to become involved in parish programs of uncertain demands and unending expectations.

5. UNITY IN RENEWAL

The various committees could hold open meetings at which all parishioners would have the opportunity to present their views and to offer their services wherever needed. The elected chairmen of the various committees and possibly one or two representative delegates from each committee would constitute a parish board which would regularly meet with the pastor to review the affairs of the parish. A record of each meeting would be published for all parishioners and there would be three or four open meetings every year to which all parishioners would be invited. The decisions of the parish board would be subject to final review and possible veto by the pastor, but each veto would be subject to review by the bishop on the occasion of his annual attendance at a board meeting.[16]

6. THE NEW ROLE OF THE PASTOR

The format of parish renewal presented in this composite construction of present and possible future efforts at parish renewal

16. "In a parish it should not be the curates and the pastor alone who are in charge of the salvation of souls. Really, it should be the laity and the nuns and the priests all together in a community sort of co-responsibility, all taking together the charge of bringing Christ to the parish, to the diocese, to the world. That is collegiality in action."—Leon Joseph Cardinal Suenens, *The Church in Dialogue* (Notre Dame, Ind.: Fides, 1965), p. 116.

may raise a pertinent question. Does it deprive the pastor of his proper role as shepherd and guide to the faithful?

It shouldn't. The pastor remains the key member of the parish who through the competent exercise of his own ministry makes the wisdom and the direction of the bishop present in each particular community. There are obvious advantages to freeing the pastor from unnecessary involvement in the administrative details of institutional management.[17] The absorption in the minor details of administration which often robs him of his time and dissipates his energy would be avoided by permitting these matters to be handled competently and efficiently by others. In a pattern of shared responsibility within the parish a pastor's administrative function could be confined to a review of major decisions made on the basis of consultation with qualified advisors, while leaving other matters of less significance to be determined by various departments. Vatican II has specifically indicated the ideal of a board of lay consultors in the administration of ecclesiastical finances.

> Ecclesiastical goods, properly so called, according to their nature and ecclesiastical law, should be administered by priests with the help of capable laymen as far as possible and should always be employed for those purposes in the pursuit of which it is licit for the Church to possess temporal goods—namely, for the carrying out of divine worship, for the procuring of honest sustenance for the clergy, and for the exercise of the works of the holy apostolate or works of charity, especially in behalf of the needy (DPL 17).

The delegation of administrative responsibility would also provide the clergy with the opportunity to give increased

17. "Priests are sometimes lecturers too, or officials in ecclesiastical administration, or politicians, scholars, writers, ascetics or many other things besides. They may be all this to such a point that other people—or even they themselves—may come to ignore the priest in them without their immediately having to cease being able to regard themselves as competent lecturers, chancery officials, scholars, writers, etc. But if a parish priest stops being in a genuine and living sense a priest, it is all over, from that same moment and to that same extent, with his existence as a pastor"—Karl Rahner, *Theology for Renewal* (New York: Sheed and Ward, 1964), p. 32.

thought and attention to their role as advisors to individuals and groups engaged in apostolic efforts. Sermons and conversations would become more effective as a result of the availability of additional time and energy for a continuing analysis of the situation in which the Gospel message is presented. Within a pattern of delegated responsibility each priest could confine—and thereby intensify—his efforts to his specifically priestly ministry, without dissipating his efforts in administrative concerns.

A listing of the advantages to be derived from devising structures of shared responsibility within a parish should not be construed as a denial of the value of past structures. The American parish has undoubtedly succeeded in developing the spiritual potential of its members and in coordinating a vast amount of apostolic commitment within its inherited framework. But the question we must now face is whether the present structure can retain its value *indefinitely*. Will we continue to have parishes of committed individuals without the bestowal of that degree of responsibility and initiative which is commensurate with the individual's growing awareness of his potential value within the Church? It would seem to be unrealistic to expect the authoritarian pattern of past efforts at coordination to retain its effectiveness in an era and an environment in which collective responsibility has proven its value and has become the accepted norm within daily life.[18]

Of course a change in the structure and administration of parish life would not be an automatic wonder worker. New patterns of responsibility will be effective only if the people involved in them are capable individuals willing to bring their talent and their time to the service of the parish. But it is a safe presump-

18. "They [ecclesiastical authorities] should entrust the layman with tasks that he can perform as well or even better than the priest, and allow him to act freely and exercise personal responsibility within the limits set for his work or demanded by the common welfare of the Church"—Pope Pius XII, "The Lay Apostolate," an address to the Second World Congress for the Lay Apostolate, October 5, 1957, *The Pope Speaks*, IV (Autumn, 1957), p. 123.

tion that the American Church has a vast, untapped reservoir of skill and wisdom in its laity. One of the basic phenomena of twentieth century American Catholicism is the rising crescendo of lay insistence on personal involvement in the life of the Church. The obvious results have been a gradual build-up of apostolic concern and activity in those areas affected by lay apostolates. There has also been a steady increase of tension within the Church as new energy contends with old patterns of direction.

The sources of tension are not difficult to determine. In hundreds of institutions the Church has been training and inspiring thousands to accept apostolic commitments at a time when in many of our parishes there are no structures to permit the utilization of these trained personnel. The seriousness of the problem is further intensified by the fact that in the documents of Vatican II the Church has clearly indicated what it should be doing in the world. Tension will be inevitable in many areas as the faithful, clergy and laity alike, compare the ideal stated in the documents with the level of execution in their own locale. Cooperation in transferring the conciliar documents into day-to-day parish life will require a sense of shared responsibility and a fraternal attitude rather different from the concentrated responsibility and the paternalism so deeply rooted in the institutions and language of the Church and in the mentality of many of its members.[19]

Would new structures encouraging the development of

19. " 'It is so much easier to do something *for* another than to do it *with* him,' writes Cardinal Suenens in *The Gospel to Every Creature,* 'to solve a problem for him than to make him discover the solution for himself and to work with him at applying the result. It is essential for a priest not to assume an authoritarian attitude, he must trust the resources of the laity. He must resist the temptation to do everything himself, on the plea that all will be better and more quickly done; he must learn how to inspire others and efface himself; in a word, to be all and to be nothing . . . Control is no doubt indispensable; control, however, does not mean repression; but rather stimulation, guidance, encouragement' "—Meyer, *The Whole World is My Neighbor,* pp. 228-229.

shared responsibility succeed in eliminating tension? It is not likely, nor would it even be desirable. A certain level of tension within the Church is needed as a stimulant to a constant reassessment of the value of current efforts and as a prompter to initiative. The problem is rather to reduce *unnecessary* tension. In order to achieve this it would seem desirable that each parish be so structured as to permit the maximum outlet of the apostolic energy of its membership. There is no common formula or format that would be effective in every case, but the goal of each parish should be a structuring of its inner life that will positively encourage and constructively utilize the apostolic potential of each member.

This structuring requires both the faith to look for charismatic gifts among the membership and the common sense to recognize that parishioners must be granted responsibility if they are expected to act as leaders. Past experience should have made it clear by now that the establishment of parish boards with little or no responsibility creates a situation where those inclined to exercise little or no initiative assume board positions without producing any noticeable change in the traditional state of affairs.

We will also need the willingness to learn from the representative structuring of other Christian communities, whose established methods of lay involvement should be considered in our efforts to form patterns of shared responsibility. Elements of Congregational and Presbyterian structures could be utilized in the formation of similar patterns within our own parish life; it is also possible that many of these communities would wish to examine our episcopal organization and its benefit as a point of coordination and independent review of parish efforts.[20]

Would it be possible to utilize the immense lay potential of

20. " . . . it could very well be possible that we others might find more to learn from the Roman Church than Rome for its part would have to learn from us, as we still assume with undue self-satisfaction"—Karl Barth, "Thoughts on the Second Vatican Council," *Ecumenical Review*, XV (July, 1963), p. 365.

our parishes without any specific form or structure? It would seem unlikely. In a de-Christianized area with relatively few committed Christians it is possible to direct a Christian response on a formless basis. But in the developed form of Catholicism in the American Church it would seem that the effective utilization of the great reservoir of lay energy will require a carefully planned assessment of resources and inclinations followed by a specific coordination of responsibility and expenditure of energy. Without a structure permitting this process to occur it is possible that the vast apostolic potential can be dissipated into low-return, energy wasting efforts. With an appropriate structure the same potential can be channeled into productive efforts capable of transforming life both within the parish and within the community.[21]

7. "MY NEW CURATE"

The development of structures encouraging the laity to exercise their true role could be paralleled by similar efforts on behalf of the parish clergy. The practice of initiating various types of creative experimentation (for example, evening Masses in homes or apartments within a parish)[22] could be regarded as a pastoral function. New emphasis could be given to the pastor's presiding

21. "The Church must organize some sort of appropriate contact with every single soul in the diocese or in the parish. Such a division of work, which we need not here discuss in detail, implies organizing; if the work is organized, there will be definite tasks, care will be taken that the output is satisfactory, a certain control will be exercised. A formless intermittent good intention is not sufficient; steam is nothing but vapor as long as we merely set water boiling"—Cardinal Suenens, *The Church in Dialogue*, p. 89.

22. A program, inaugurated by Bishop Loras T. Lane of Rockford, permits priests of the diocese to say Mass in homes of their parishioners. Two pastors have divided their parishes into districts made up of from 12 to 126 families. A Mass will be celebrated in each district until a service has been held in all of the neighborhoods within the parish boundaries. A social gathering follows each Mass, allowing the parishioners, their guests, and the parish priest an opportunity to become acquainted—*Baltimore Catholic Review*, Oct. 29, 1965.

role within the community by permitting him to ordain to minor
orders the young men in the parish studying for the priesthood.
He would also preside at the annual profession of vows by sisters from the parish. Both functions would make clear to the
parish its contribution to the universal Church and would also
develop a sense of solidarity among religious and laity which is
not attained when these rites occur outside the parish.

A time and motion study of the work load performed by
pastor and assistant priests within a parish during a determined
period of time would undoubtedly reveal that a great deal of
priestly time is necessarily consumed in non-priestly work.[23] If
such a study could be made in an adequate sampling of parishes
within a diocese the results might lead to efforts designed to
free priests of minor duties not related to their ministry. The
utilization of the services of married deacons and lay theologians within a parish would suggest new patterns in the assigning of priests.[24] It is possible that one priest assisted by a team
of laity could adequately staff a parish inefficiently utilizing two
or three priests at the present time. Priests reassigned from
either minimal return or low-yield situations could serve in areas
of the greatest need and the highest return as determined by a
comparative analysis of priestly involvement over a period of
time. The necessity of providing a number of Sunday Masses in
larger parishes would continue to require the availability of
several priests on that day until such time as these parishes

23. Fichter found that parish priests spend a significant amount of time
in functions which they do not regard as highly satisfying and for which
they feel they were not adequately prepared; directing organizations and
financial administration were respectively second and third on the list of
time-consuming functions, but only eighth and ninth in the list of satis-
faction-producing and best prepared roles. Although the priests preferred
to serve as spiritual fathers and counsellors, the execution of these roles
was limited by involvement in administrative functions—*Priest and People,*
pp. 184 ff.

24. For a progress report on the work of lay theologians, see James G.
Dowling, "Lay Theologians in the Parishes," *Shield,* Oct.-Nov., 1964.

could be divided into smaller units. But in the meantime there would appear to be only minimal value in confining the week-day involvement of the clergy to a single location unless there is a definite advantage being gained by this practice.

Various forms of experimentation could be tried to determine the most effective location for the parish clergy. Should three or four priests share a common residence or should each priest live in a particular section of the parish entrusted entirely to his care? Does one priest have to be pastor and the other priests have to be assistants, or would it be possible to establish parishes with three priests acting according to a pattern of majority decision?[25] Today's inner-city parish obviously requires both a mentality and a special competence on the part of its clergy which might be best obtained by permitting volunteer clerical teams to apply for a collective assignment to particular parishes.[26] Consideration could also be given to establishing four or five member teams of priests with a specialized ministry, such as civil rights or industrial missions.

It is also necessary that attention be given to establishing significant new roles for the younger clergy. In certain dioceses a priest may spend twenty or thirty years or possibly a lifetime in the role of an assistant; his individual powers of initiative and independent decision frequently atrophy long before he receives his own pastorate.[27] Is there a single diocese in the United States which uses a professional method of determining the various abilities of priests and assigns them to positions on the basis of indicated competence? The practice of making assignments and transfers without any discernible meaningfulness frequently

25. Cf. Daniel J. Mallette, "In the Inner City," *Commonweal*, March 25, 1966. Father Mallette works with two other priests on a "team" basis in an experimental inner city parish in Chicago.

26. Cardinal Ritter of St. Louis has indicated his willingness to consider volunteers for inner city assignments.

27. "Let no one deny that the trauma of frustrated assistants is serious in the Church. Our present, almost universal system of inefficient utilization of personnel prevents them from exercising their charismata now and

results in giving the lower clergy the impression that they are faceless, interchangeable parts.

> Thoughtful care should be given to the spiritual life [of priests] as well as their mental and bodily welfare, and, so far as it is possible, the circumstances and conditions of labor should be adapted to individual needs and capabilities (DCP 10).

It is interesting to note that seniority, a predominant factor in appointment to pastoral positions in the American Church, was not cited by the council fathers in their listing of qualifications for determining assignments.

> In forming a judgment on the suitability of a priest for the administration of any parish the bishop should take into consideration not only his knowledge of doctrine but also his piety, apostolic zeal and other gifts and qualities which are necessary for the proper exercise of the care of souls (DCP 31).

The need for a professional analysis of each priest's aptitude and inclinations, a policy of consulting priests regarding future appointments, the establishment of an adequate pension fund and equitable salaries for priests,[28] and the formation of open lines of communication between bishop and priests would be matters requiring discussion by the representative senate of

---

unfits them to do so when and if they become pastors"—Bishop Stephen A. Leven at the Vatican Council, Oct. 16, 1964.

28. In some areas a priest in an affluent parish may be receiving an income two or three times greater than a neighboring priest whose salary is frequently insufficient to meet his personal expenses. For a proposed method of correcting current imbalances in clerical salaries, see C. Walter Weiss, "The Priest's Salary," *The Homiletic and Pastoral Review,* March, 1964. This question also involves, of course, the whole complicated question of stipends. This is not only a practical question. The whole theology of stipends is in need of review.

priests which the council fathers have directed each bishop to establish in his diocese.[29]

> The bishop should regard priests as his brothers and friends. As far as in him lies he should have at heart the material and especially spiritual welfare of his priests. For above all, upon the bishop rests the heavy responsibility for the sanctity of his priests. Hence, he should exercise the greatest care on behalf of the continual formation of his priests. He should gladly listen to them, indeed, consult them, and have discussions with them about those matters which concern the necessities of pastoral work and the welfare of the diocese.
>
> In order to put these ideals into effect, a group or senate of priests representing the presbytery should be established. It is to operate in a manner adapted to modern circumstances and needs and have a form and norms to be determined by law. By its counsel, this body will be able to give effective assistance to the bishop in the government of his diocese (DPL 7).

If the senate of priests is to be truly representative of all the priests of a diocese as intended by the council, it would seem essential that its members be elected by all the priests for fixed terms at periodic intervals. In this manner the decisionary influence of appointive chancery officials would be balanced by the fresh insights of priest-representatives of the entire diocesan clergy.[30]

Attention should also be given to the post-ordination devel-

29. Bishop John J. Wright has also announced the organization of a clergy council, established to improve communication between the chancery and the diocesan clergy and to serve as a forum for discussing common problems. The priest representatives are elected by the clergy of their deaneries, and meet at least four times a year with the bishop. Members must be ordained at least five years and must not be deans, diocesan consultors or heads of any diocesan departments.

30. The trend in American dioceses seems to be to recognize the value of electing priests to the pastoral senate or council; Washington, D. C., Manchester, N. H., Newark, N. J., and Lincoln, Nebr. are among those dioceses which now elect priests to some form of diocesan council.

opment of the professional abilities and inclinations of priests, a process which too frequently depends almost entirely on the spontaneous efforts of priests themselves.[31] In this regard it would seem advisable that bishops adopt for their diocesan clergy the policy which the council recommends for religious superiors.

> Religious should strive during the whole course of their lives to perfect the culture they have received in matters spiritual and in arts and sciences. Likewise, superiors must, as far as this is possible, obtain for them the opportunity, equipment and time to do this (DOA 18).

The problem of adequate communication between bishops and priests would appear to be approaching the status of a crisis when one examines its growing dimensions. When a priest of unquestioned integrity and zeal is in open disagreement with his superiors the case frequently becomes a matter of public attention.[32] The trend to give widespread publicity to outstanding examples of conscientious disagreement within the Church can be expected to increase as the laity and clergy concerned about the issues involved develop experience and skill in the techniques of public protest, such as full page ads in the *New York Times* questioning the procedures involved in the unexpected transfer of Father Daniel Berrigan, S.J., from New York to South America.

31. In an archdiocesan training program directed by Father Theodore C. Stone, the Archdiocese of Chicago is divided into seven areas and the clergy meet on a regular basis in fifty different centers. Other dioceses, e.g., St. Paul, use the diocesan seminary as a center for post-ordination programs for the clergy.

32. Cf. "The Silenced Priests," *Ave Maria,* January 8, 1966. *Ave Maria* lists eleven case histories (Fathers William DuBay, Joel Moelter, O.Carm., J. Clement Burns, O.P., John V. Coffield, Philip Berrigan, S.S.J., Philip E. Berryman, Maurice Ouellet, S.S.D., Gommar DePauw, James E. Groppi, Bonaventure O'Brien, O.F.M., and Daniel Berrigan, S.J.) during the eighteen-month period between June, 1964 and November, 1965. For the comments of men and women exercising authority in the church, see *Ave Maria,* Feb. 20, 1966.

Would these incidents occur so frequently if there were better lines of communication between priests and superiors? Certainly the individual priest whose conscience directs him to a commitment not endorsed by his bishop deserves an objective analysis of his position by a group of his peers rather than an arbitrary pronouncement by the authority involved. This would not deny the bishop's or the superior's competence to pass final judgment on individual cases, but what is needed is an impartial, collective consideration of the evidence on behalf of the individual's dissent prior to the superior's decision in his regard.[33] It seems likely that most bishops would greatly appreciate the services of an impartial board in making recommendations regarding conscientious dissent. The establishment of scrupulously objective standards of judgment and their application to individual cases by a peer group of clergy and laity of recognized competence would greatly assist in the process of providing justice to individuals and would also protect the Church from the unpleasant consequences of human arbitrariness. In the *Declaration on Religious Freedom* the council has clearly indicated the freedom which the Church should have.

> Among the things that concern the good of the Church and indeed the welfare of society here on earth—things therefore that are always and everywhere to be kept secure and defended against all injury—this certainly is preeminent, namely, that the Church should enjoy that full measure of freedom which her care for the salvation of men requires (DRF 13).

Public opinion will now be closely observing the Church to see whether it in turn will provide its ministers with the full measure of freedom which their care for the salvation of men requires.

---

33. "The Superior has the final decision, the last word—but not the second-last word. It is normal and sensible that subordinates be asked for and give their views before a decision is made"—Leon Cardinal Suenens, *The Nun in the World*, p. 139.

The suggestion of Father William Dubay to unionize the diocesan clergy is an understandable form of response to a situation in which authority presents itself as an employer.[34] It would be unfortunate for the Church if the misuse of authority were to harden the bishop-priest relationship into a pattern similar to the employer-union relationship. Vatican II has stated a different ideal.

> They [the bishops] should regard the priests as sons and friends and be ready to listen to them. Through their trusting familiarity with their priests they should strive to promote the whole pastoral work of the entire diocese (DCP 16).

> All presbyters, both diocesan and religious, participate in and exercise with the bishop the one priesthood of Christ and are thereby constituted prudent cooperators of the episcopal order. . . . In consequence, they form one presbytery and one family whose father is the bishop (DCP 28).

The most successful business enterprises have long been adept

34. Father William DuBay has listed ten demands the priests' union might make: 1) tenure policy which would guarantee a priest a fair hearing by his peers before he was suspended; 2) due process through a grievance machinery; 3) freedom from arbitrary and oppressive transfers from one parish to another; 4) freedom to preach; 5) uniform policy for taking leaves of absence; 6) open personnel files; 7) freedom to live where he pleases; 8) fair promotional policies, not dependent on episcopal favoritism or whim; 9) a salary policy that would make it unnecessary to depend on the "buying and selling of religious services" and reliance on the generosity of the wealthy; and 10) definition of professional responsibilities, which would exclude the curate from such mandatory chores as money-counting, fund raising, janitorial tasks, and bookkeeping.

Father Paul Zeller has proposed that a priests' union be established within the framework of the church and regulated by canon law. Father Zeller has sent a list of proposed canonical guidelines to the special committee of the Canon Law Society of America currently gathering suggestions for the revamping of canon law. According to his guidelines, all priests would be eligible for membership in a diocesan-wide union. The union's elected officers would be canonically authorized to represent priests singly and collectively. If bishops rejected their representation, the union would have the right to appeal to a higher authority—*National Catholic Reporter,* April 20, 1966.

at developing techniques of representative consultation through encouragement of personal encounters within their organization and by providing open forums and periodic questionnaires to detemine general attitudes. The reluctance to transfer these successful procedures to ecclesiastical affairs or even to recognize the value of any form of communication has produced a growing amount of irritation among the lower clergy in recent years to which ecclesiastical administrators seem oblivious, but which perceptive laity have recognized as a coming crisis. The council fathers have indicated a procedure by which the crisis can be averted.

> The relationships between the bishop and the diocesan priests should rest most especially upon the bonds of supernatural charity so that the harmony of the will of the priests with that of their bishop will render their pastoral activity more fruitful. Wherefore, for the sake of greater service to souls, let the bishop call the priests into dialogue, especially about pastoral matters. This he should do not only on a given occasion but at regularly fixed intervals insofar as this is possible (DCP 28).

Priests who have not had the benefit of open communication with their bishop will be awaiting the implementation of this summons to dialogue with the same eagerness with which the laity await the developments of their lines of communication with the clergy.[35] In one sense the willingness of bishops to establish a regular pattern of dialogue and meaningful encounters with their priests will be the great revealer of the future direction of Church life in the United States. It should not be a difficult matter for any bishop to develop personal contacts with his priests; the only requirement is the gift of episcopal time

35. Priests of the Tulsa-Oklahoma City Diocese have nominated 27 priests for membership on two commissions of the diocese's "Little Council" called by Bishop Victor J. Reed.

Cardinal Glennon sent a letter to his priests in 1911 which included blank ballots for choosing diocesan consultors.—St. Louis Review, Vol. XXV, No. 28.

and attention where it is most needed.[36] If there is a general willingness on the part of the hierarchy to listen to priests it is very likely that the listening process will be expanded to include the entire body of the faithful. But if the bishop's door is closed to his priests it is not likely that it will be opened to many of the faithful.

A particularly compelling problem for the American Church is the high rate of departure of personnel from the clerical life. By conservative estimate there are between four and five thousand priests or approximately ten percent of ordained personnel who have relinquished the practice of their priestly office.[37] Although there are a variety of explanations given for this phenomenon, such as frustration due to absence of understanding and communication, there is no reliable evidence as to the nature or the extent of the occupational hazards of priestly life responsible for this high departure rate. Research into the situation is obviously needed to determine accurately the factors resulting in current losses and to offer guidelines to correct whatever situations are found to be responsible. It will also be necessary to establish additional institutes to help priests in need of assistance and those priests who wish to return to the practice of their profes-

36. On the basis of a questionnaire sent to all the priests of the Tulsa-Oklahoma City Diocese a document has been prepared which proposes several changes in current clerical structures. The proposals include putting clergy assignments on a rotating basis; replacing the ordinary pastor-curate relationship with a system of associate pastors, co-pastors, or pastoral teams; establishing a diocesan personnel commission on lay and clerical manpower, and limiting the ordinary tenure of pastors to from five to seven years—*The Oklahoma Courier,* June 10, 1966.

37. *Time* (Vol. 84, Aug. 21, 1964, p. 40) reported that there were between 4,000 and 5,000 priests who have left the clergy in the U. S. with frustration high among their reasons. "Because of information received from confidential sources which I consider reliable, I believe that Time's estimate is generally accurate."—Stafford Poole, *Seminary in Crisis* (New York: Herder and Herder, 1965), p. 171. For an analysis of the problem, see Joseph H. Fichter, S.J., *Religion as an Occupation* (Notre Dame, 1961), pp. 204-210.

sion. The problem has reached the stage where it cannot be confined to closed door discussions; the faithful who find the problem presented in the secular press will be looking to the Church for a solution.[38] The official Church's willingness to investigate objectively the dimensions of the difficulties of its priests and its subsequent decision to act with justice and charity to alleviate the problem will be a real test of its courage and its integrity in the face of inner difficulty.

Recognition of the validity of the marriages of former priests would be a vital first step in the more humane treatment of those who have a special right to the justice of the Church; it is difficult to see the wisdom in denying the sacraments to a man who may have spent ten or twenty years in administering them to others simply on the basis of his marriage. In this regard it should be noted that the presence of married deacons within the postconciliar Church will probably lead to a complete reappraisal of the practice of priestly celibacy. The reasons for asking priests to be celibate in the twentieth century are not the same as those which first prompted the law of priestly celibacy established in the fourth century (but never really effective on a wide scale until the twelfth century).[39]

It is important to recall that although the early Christians placed a high value on virginity they did not link it with the office of priesthood; in the early centuries many of the clergy practiced celibacy voluntarily but no one questioned the zeal or the availability of the majority of the clergy who married. Many of the reasons advanced to justify the present practice of

38. Cf. Sanche de Gramont, "Fallen Priests," *Saturday Evening Post,* May 1, 1965, and "Whiskey Priests," *Newsweek,* Jan. 10, 1966.

39. Cf. David P. O'Neill, *Priestly Celibacy and Maturity* (New York: Sheed and Ward, 1965). In his consideration of priestly celibacy in the Western Church, Father O'Neill finds it significant that no law linked celibacy and priesthood until the local Council of Elvira imposed celibacy on priests in the fourth century. The practice was not made definitive on a world-wide basis until the First Lateran Council in 1123.

a celibate clergy would probably be regarded as oddly irrelevant by Christians of other eras.[40]

The question of celibacy today deserves to receive intensive research and analysis from a wide variety of viewpoints—historical, psychological, theological, ascetical. It would be a grave mistake to base the case for priestly celibacy on views that are pseudo-practical (the priest would be distracted from his duties by family life) or pseudo-mystical (a married priest could not give as much love to his people as a celibate priest). These views ignore the fact that Christ and the early Church did not use the criterion of celibacy in the selection of ministers and that the power to love others is generally intensified rather than diminished by affection for those bound within the family. They also constitute an implicit denial of the value of the current practice of Orthodox and Protestant ministers. There are good reasons for celibacy today and they deserve to constitute the basis of discussion.

> Celibacy has a many-faceted suitability for the priesthood. For the whole priestly mission is dedicated to the service of a new humanity which Christ, the victor over death, has aroused through His Spirit in the world and which has its origin "not of blood, nor of the will of the flesh, nor of the will of man but of God." Through virginity, then, or celibacy observed for the Kingdom of Heaven, priests are consecrated to Christ by a new and exceptional reason. . . . In this way they profess themselves before men as willing to be dedicated to the office committed to them—namely, to commit themselves faithfully to one man and to show themselves as a chaste virgin for Christ and thus to evoke the mysterious marriage established by Christ, and fully to be manifested in the future, in which the Church has Christ as her only Spouse. They give, moreover, a living sign of the world to come, by a faith and charity already made

40. Cf. "Celibacy," *The Catholic Encyclopedia* (New York: Robert Appleton Company, 1907).

present, in which the children of the resurrection neither marry nor take wives (DPL 16).

Chastity not only symbolizes in a singular way the heavenly goods but also the most suitable means by which religious dedicate themselves with undivided heart to the service of God and the works of the apostolate. In this way they recall to the minds of all the faithful that wondrous marriage decreed by God and which is to be fully revealed in the future age in which the Church takes Christ as its only Spouse (DOA 12).

Perhaps the Church will decide eventually to return to the practice of earlier ages when celibacy was accepted by the clergy on its own merits without an ecclesiastical edict on the matter. But it will be difficult to decide the relative merits of a celibate or a married clergy in a purely hypothetical manner without an actual basis of comparison. Experimentation with a married clergy in areas where priests are scarce and limited experiments with a married clergy in other areas may offer the only satisfactory determination of the matter. In the meantime it will be helpful to adopt a completely open approach to the question.

Indeed, it [celibacy] is not demanded by the very nature of the priesthood, as is apparent from the practice of the early Church and from the traditions of the Eastern Churches, where besides those who with all the bishops, by a gift of grace, chose to observe celibacy, there are also married priests of the highest merit (DPL 16).

If the nature of the priesthood does not *demand* celibacy, does the current practice of the Church and its historical recognition of celibacy as an ideal indicate an affinity or intimate tendency of unity between priesthood and celibacy? Ida Gorres believes that only gradually does the Church come to realizations such as the awareness that a celibate priesthood is the form most expressive of Christ's priesthood which must be lived totally.[41] If this is true, if there is an authentic, inner affinity between priesthood and celibacy, then the western Church's current practice of accepting priests on condition that they possess the charism of celibacy may constitute an inspired development in the process of the Church's growing awareness of itself.

But if the relationship between priesthood and celibacy is purely an external relationship historically determined by environmental and cultural considerations, it will be necessary to consider alternatives to the inherited tradition of a celibate clergy. Father David P. O'Neill has suggested that candidates to the priesthood be given the opportunity of exercising a five-year active diaconate immediately prior to ordination. During this period the candidate would be free to marry and continue his ministry as a married deacon. If after a five-year diaconate the candidate chose celibacy he could choose the priestly ministry. Father O'Neill believes that after this type of mature choice it would be a relatively rare occurrence for a priest subsequently to choose marriage. But in the event that he did, he could continue his ministry as a married priest.

In the post-conciliar age is there any reason why a married priesthood would not be as acceptable as the married diaconate authorized by the council? Only time and an openness to both discussion and experimentation will reveal to what extent celibacy should be an ideal associated with the priestly role.[42] The discussion will inevitably influence our total rethinking of the role of the Christian priest in our world.

41. Ida Friederike Goerres, *Is Celibacy Outdated?* (Westminster: Newman, 1965).

42. For a comprehensive study of the issues involved in the discussion of clerical celibacy, see R. J. Bunnik, "The Question of Married Priests," in *Cross Currents,* Fall, 1965 and Winter, 1965.

Chapter Three

THE CHURCH AT THE GRASS ROOTS: THE PARISH—FUNCTIONS AND MEMBERS

Reorganization of the parish must ultimately be based, not on some abstract ideal, but on a practical re-evaluation of its functions by its members.The Church is actively present to the world through the parish, the local Church, and the individuals who make it up. As post-conciliar Catholics respond to their essential role in the total life of the Church, and their responsibility as Christians to the whole human community, careful study is required of the real needs and responsibilities of the members of the parish and of the wider community which the parish is called to serve. One major element of present parish life that requires study is, of course, the parish school.

1. TO SCHOOL OR NOT TO SCHOOL

At the 1964 convention of the National Catholic Educational Association the Elementary School Department offered $40,000 to anyone who would document the "success story" of the parochial school. The fund and the potential book were obviously intended as a rebuttal to Mary Perkins Ryan's *Are Parochial Schools the Answer?* In one sense it is unfortunate that the Elementary School Department did not present the $40,000 to Mrs. Ryan. Her questioning and the questioning of other critics of the schools perform a vital service to Catholic education which deserves some form of official remuneration.

The irritation of the school personnel over Mrs. Ryan's controversial book was understandable. She had challenged the value of their work by contending that on the basis of their immense involvement of personnel and finances the schools could not be considered as especially successful in their program of religious formation and that perhaps some other method of formation could achieve better results. There was not much point in criticizing Mrs. Ryan for not producing evidence to support her criticism; there was really none available to question or to vindicate the overall achievement of the school system.[1]

Why this absence of data? For years the general impression had been that the schools were eminently effective in religious formation; extensive research was not required to establish the obvious. There had been questionnaires circulated, doctoral dissertations written and statistics collected on various aspects of the school program but there had been no comprehensive analysis of the entire system offering an accurate evaluation of its overall effectiveness.[2]

It is unfortunate that despite the questioning of the precise value of the schools by Mrs. Ryan and other critics (a vital service for which the critics are rarely thanked), the hierarchy has

1. For a discussion of the inadequacy of sociological data regarding American Catholicism, see Andrew Greeley, "Sociology and Religion," *The Critic*, Aug.-Sept., 1962.

For a scientific study of a parochial school as a social unit, see Joseph H. Fichter, S.J., *Parochial School: A Sociological Study* (Garden City: Anchor, 1964). The work of Fathers Fichter and Greeley represents pioneering efforts in the field of religious sociology for the American Catholic Church.

2. "In the past the schools got by because no one took the trouble, or dared, to measure their actual results. Pietistic support was the rule. That rule must be changed. The sociologists can help by finding out what the schools actually achieve. The theologians can help by clarifying the ends of a Christian education. But the last word must come from the Christian conscience"—Daniel Callahan, "The Schools," *Commonweal*, Jan. 8, 1965.

not yet displayed its determination to finance the necessary analysis of the actual accomplishments of the schools. Although more than five million children (approximately 15 percent of United States children of school age) attend Catholic schools, the discussion of their value has been conducted without an appreciable amount of factual information regarding their actual effects. Two studies financed by the Carnegie Foundation have now provided some helpful data.[3]

The first Carnegie-supported study was intended to describe the present status of the schools, operation, organization, financing, and so on.[4] The study compiled nationwide statistics, made special studies of 322 selected schools in 13 dioceses in different parts of the nation, and analyzed questionnaires returned by 27,000 parents regarding their expectations of the schools. Some of the significant findings:

1. Academic achievement of pupils in Catholic schools is significantly higher than national norms.

2. Enrollment in Catholic schools tends to be more selective in the acceptance and retaining of students, a factor contributing to the higher academic status of the schools.

3. Catholic parents give a high rate of support to the general objectives of Catholic schools.

4. The ten most important expectations of parents for Catholic schools (listed in the order of their frequency of response) are: To be honest, truthful, and moral; to teach knowledge of God, Christ and the Church; to train children in the practice of their religion; to teach the child to think for himself; to have qualified sisters, priests, etc., as teachers; to train the

3. For a summary of the results of the Carnegie-supported studies see *Carnegie Corporation of New York Quarterly*, April, 1965.

4. Under the auspices of the University of Notre Dame, it was directed by Reginald A. Neuwien, former superintendent of schools in Stanford, Connecticut, and was under the general leadership of Rev. Theodore M. Hesburg, president of Notre Dame, Msgr. Frederick G. Hochwalt, executive secretary of the National Catholic Educational Association, and George N. Shuster, former president of Hunter College in New York.

child in respect for persons and property; to teach him to read and write well; to train him in citizenship; to have qualified lay teachers; to have space for all Catholic children.

5. Parents do not consider the schools to be overly taxing financially in view of their value.

6. Parents believe that the religious goals of teaching and training in the faith are those most successfully achieved by the schools.

7. The median salary of all lay teachers is $4,200.00, while the average beginning salary of public school teachers is $4,600.00.

8. The status of the lay teacher in Catholic schools has improved but it has not reached equality with the religious teacher.

9. In the six-year period from 1962 to 1968 it would be necessary to increase enrollment by 748,700 to maintain the percentage of Catholic children in Catholic schools.

The second Carnegie study was conducted by the University of Chicago's National Opinion Research Center (NORC).[5] The study attempted to measure the effects Catholic education has on the later social and religious attitudes of its students. Data for the investigation were obtained through personal interviews with a representative national sample of 2,753 American Catholics between the ages of 23 and 57, and from questionnaires returned from an additional 1,000 respondents, all the adolescents in the homes of sampled families, and a randomly selected sample of 1,000 *Commonweal* readers. Some of the findings include:

1. Catholics who attended Catholic schools score slightly

5. The NORC investigation was under the direction of Peter Rossi, head of the Center, Rev. Andrew Greeley, director of the study, and Leonard J. Pinto, associate director. Results of the study on the effects of Catholic education were reported by Dr. Rossi, Father Greeley and Dr. Pinto in *The Critic*, Dec., 1963, Oct., 1964, and Feb.-March, 1965. See also Greeley and Rossi, *The Education of Catholic Americans* (Aldine, 1966).

higher on various measures of religious belief and behavior and tend to be more doctrinally and ethically orthodox in matters such as papal primacy and sexual morality.

2. The schools seem to have been most successful at inculcating those norms already reasonably well accepted among American Catholics, especially those matters of creed and code which served as important characteristics to immigrant Catholics in a hostile environment. The schools were also successful in establishing standards important to the Church of the nineteenth century, e.g., attendance at Mass, sexual morality, acceptance of authority.

3. In the areas of social justice and civil liberties, attendance at Catholic schools was of less importance than the amount of education.

4. Those with all their schooling under Catholic auspices were significantly less anti-semitic and racist than secular-educated Catholics.

5. The greatest religious influence of the schools occurred for those students who attended Catholic colleges after Catholic primary and secondary schools, and whose families possessed a high degree of religiousness.

6. Attendance at a Catholic college after *public* grade and high schools apparently has little effect, even in such areas as rejection of religious extremism and concern for civil liberties.

7. No evidence was discovered to show that the schools have had a harmful effect on civic behavior, or that they create divisiveness, or that they handicap the social or economic success of those who attend them.

8. The study did not substantiate the idea that the apparent vitality of Catholicism in the United States is the result of the parochial school system. The schools could be considered *the result of the vitality* and it is possible that, if there were no parochial schools, American Catholicism would not be overwhelmingly different from what it is today.

It is possible to evaluate the sociological data uncovered by the two studies in radically different ways, depending on the effects expected of the schools. Those who regard as valuable the inculcation of fixed standards of creed and code will regard the Carnegie studies as supporting their position. Those who have criticized the schools on the failure to communicate a more dynamic vision of Christian life and Catholic responsibility will also have their viewpoint reinforced.[6]

It is fortunate that no decision is being made regarding the relative effectiveness of Catholic primary, secondary and higher education on the basis of information obtained so far. No one is now in a position to decide Whether Parochial Schools Are the Answer.[7] But should this condition continue? Is it reasonable to continue the vast program of Catholic education without additional intense research energetically supported and adequately financed by the Church itself?

The Carnegie Foundation studies can not be considered conclusive. A considerable amount of additional research will be necessary to determine accurately the religious and academic value of the Catholic school system. But research requires money and up to now the hierarchy has hesitated to make the necessary expenditures. It is a curious fact that although the recent criticism directed toward the schools has provoked a large quantity of counter-criticism on the part of authority it has not provoked any sizeable outlay of research funds to vindicate objectively what is being questioned. Yet research is vital if we are to

6. Callahan, "The Schools," *Commonweal*, Jan. 8, 1965.
7. "This, then, is the kind of instruction we need to plan for—one by its very nature centered in the Church, rather than in the school, and calling for personal thought and effort rather than 'indoctrination.' It will therefore be the work of the pastor, the parent, and the 'coach' in Christian living rather than that simply of the classroom teacher. And it is in relation to the aim of making such instruction and formation available to all Catholics that we need to evaluate our present means of instruction and our Catholic school system as a whole"—Mary Perkins Ryan, *Are Parochial Schools the Answer?* (New York: Holt, Rinehart and Winston, 1964), p. 112.

secure an adequate return on the approximately two billion dollars already invested in the school system.

The self-evaluation programs recently adopted by many elementary and secondary schools undoubtedly offer the participating schools an evaluation of their curriculum, teaching staff, and facilities, but they do not offer anything resembling a scientific analysis of the comprehensive value of a particular school system or the post-school results of its religious formation program. Only research teams operating on a nationwide basis and supported by funds sufficient to secure a detailed analysis can present a reliable evaluation of both the value of the national program of religious formation and the ultimate effectiveness of the schools.

It would seem that some of the questions recently raised regarding the pattern and the direction of educational efforts could reasonably be expected to receive the initial attention of research programs. A partial listing might include the following items:

1. Since it is obvious that we cannot give a Catholic education to every student, at what age and in what department (elementary, high school, college) should we concentrate our efforts?[8] It is merely avoiding the issue to say we should attempt to maintain schools "across the board" without determining to concentrate on any particular age or department; at present we concentrate our efforts in the elementary school department (approximately 75 percent of available educational resources are directed to grades 1-8) and a reluctance to make a decision regarding future concentration means that we have agreed on the basis of little or no evidence to continue the current concentration.

2. On the elementary level, do we secure an adequate

8. For a debate on the relative merits of concentrating emphasis on either Catholic elementary or Catholic high schools, see "Debate: Elementary vs. Secondary Schools," *National Catholic Educational Association Bulletin*, Aug., 1962, pp. 439 ff.

return on our educational investment by our fragmentation of resources (one parochial school in one parish) or should we establish consolidated schools (one centrally located grade school for four or five parishes) with central financing?[9] It would seem to make little sense to continue dissipating our finances and personnel into many units when various types of consolidation have demonstrated their value on other levels. But only careful comparison of different systems and scientific evaluation of the results will indicate with some degree of certainty the relative advantages of consolidation.

3. How effective are religious formation programs other than those offered by the Catholic school system? This will be difficult to determine because of the widely varying quality of the Confraternity of Christian Doctrine programs, that is, the programs of religious formation usually offered by parishes to students not attending Catholic schools. A recent nationwide survey indicated that the diocesan directors of CCD programs believe that the Catholic schools in their dioceses receive 95 percent of available resources of finances and personnel as compared with five percent left for religious formation outside the school.[10] Thus it will be difficult to secure an adequate base upon

9. Speaking at the American Association of School Administrators at Atlantic City, N. J., on Feb. 15, 1966, Professor Anthony E. Seidl of the University of Notre Dame called for major reforms in the administration and financing of Catholic schools: "To use a system of financing and an administrative organization which are basically the same as 80 years ago and had demonstrated their incompetency is unrealistic"—*The Washington Post*, Feb. 16, 1966.

10. Sixty-two archdioceses and dioceses representing approximately 40% of the nation's CCD programs participated in a survey conducted by Father Joseph O'Donoghue in April, 1964. When questioned regarding the greatest difficulty facing the CCD program, the participating CCD directors referred to the following factors, listed here in the order of frequency of their citation: 1) episcopal and pastoral apathy; 2) organizational faults (i.e., inadequate staffing, finances and policies); 3) confusion of the role of CCD when compared with that of the Catholic school; 4) lack of trained teachers; 5) perseverance in developing the full CCD program. See NCWC release, July 25, 1964.

which an objective comparison can be made of both systems (religious formation in the school, and that offered outside the school) operating at prime effectiveness. But the effort must be made in order to provide an objective basis for decision.

The results of additional research may not be pleasant to contemplate. Research could lead to a considerable loss of self-esteem as the traditional platitudes are replaced by an objective analysis of the school system's deficiencies as well as its accomplishments. An improved vision of our actual situation may reveal an over-allotment of available resources to the minority within the school system that is detrimental to the majority outside the system.[11] It may also reveal that the pattern of enormous investments of resources in Catholic institutions has an immense power of perpetuating itself beyond the point of adequate return even for those within the system.[12]

But research is bound to uncover encouraging news as well. Research at the University of Chicago has provided some support for the contention that the most significant years in a child's development are the first three years of school, during which 50 percent of the individual's skills are acquired.[13] If substantiated by additional research this finding could provide significant endorsement for the Church's heavy concentration of energy in

11. On the basis of a survey of 20,000 Catholics in California and Arizona, Father Eugene J. Schallert concluded that 85% of the parish educational dollar is being spent on less than 10% of the people to be educated. See "Catholic Parishes and Social Responsibility," *Season*, Spring, 1964.

12. "Think, finally, of the $100,000,000 (the 1960 figure) spent annually on parochial school maintenance, operation, and renovation, and of the vast sums used for the same purposes by Catholic high schools and colleges. Think of the tens of millions of dollars (the figure in 1958 was $157 million) now going each year for new construction, which would then be available instead for parish programs of religious instruction, for Newman Club work, for urgently needed services to special groups, and for all the other works of the Church in this country—as well as for missions in every other part of the world"—Ryan, *Are Parochial Schools the Answer?*, p. 164.

13. See the address of William H. Conley, president of Sacred Heart University, Bridgeport, Conn., to the Catholic Home-School Associations of Oradell, N. J., Spring, 1966.

the primary grades. Even the discovery of unpleasant facts (as that only 53 percent of the Catholic school students participating in the survey of National Opinion Research Center agreed with the statement that it is more important to love one's neighbor than to abstain from meat on Friday) may not be classified as essential defects within the system. This type of catechetical imbalance may reflect the consensus of an earlier generation regarding what should be emphasized in religious instruction. The adoption of the conciliar attitude and the development of an improved catechesis will hopefully correct inherited misconceptions and make the schools an adaptable instrument for constant renewal.

The two Carnegie studies of Catholic schools cost that foundation almost half a million dollars, an expenditure which may explain the Church's reluctance to finance research programs. But relative to the Church's current financial involvement in education, the cost of the two studies represents slightly more than the average amount spent on each day of the year in the construction of new buildings and the maintenance of existing structures. It would seem almost incredible to conceive of a situation in which the Church would continue to build without authorizing the comprehensive research necessary to measure the effectiveness of current efforts and to determine the areas of maximum return for future investments.

This research will require a base of comparison wider than that which is available at present. To provide this base efforts should be initiated to develop alternatives to the existing system. Conceivably this would include:

1. *An end to the amateur status of the CCD program by emphatically recognizing the need for salaried professionals throughout the entire program.* This would involve the regular use of salaried teachers and financial expenditures comparing favorably with those of the Catholic school in the same area. It

would also involve an objective review of the administration or lack of administration of the program in each parish by qualified personnel from an accrediting service. Failure to provide the local CCD program with teachers and adminstrative personnel with both the professional background and the financial support to improve their skill through additional training will doom to perpetual second-class status the program of religious formation outside the school. The quality of CCD program has always lagged behind that of the neighboring parochial school, and now that the sisters and lay teachers entering the school system are better trained initially and have the opportunity to add to their competency through in-service institutes and special courses, it would be unrealistic to expect the CCD program to make similar advances without a comparable endowment of salaried personnel and administration.

2. *A limited moratorium on immediate building plans to permit raising salaries to a level designed to attract the most competent teachers into the system.* Is it necessary that Catholic school enrollment should increase every year?[14] Could the money spent on new construction be more profitably directed into improving existing facilities and providing salaries which would gain the services of exceptionally qualified teachers? The willingness to forego temporarily adding a few thousand students to the system could considerably raise the opportunity level for the millions already within the system. Additional improvement could be gained by accepting talented laity into the key administerial positions generally reserved for religious: for example, the office of principal. And since there is some evidence to indicate that when all the expenses of religious are

14. Statistics released by the National Catholic Educational Association in April, 1965, indicated a total grade school enrollment of 4,541,000 and a total high school enrollment of 1,087,000 which represented respective gains of only two-tenths of one percent and two percent. The association, however, predicted increases of 1% and 3.4% in the following year—N.C.E.A. release, April 21, 1965.

tabulated lay teachers represent a smaller financial investment, it would be desirable to establish a number of schools staffed either completely or predominantly with laity to offer a base for further evaluation.[15]

3. *The adoption of various forms of consolidation of existing institutions.* What are the advantages of maintaining three convents and three schools within the radius of a mile? A single convent and a single school could be far more efficient and less expensive. But other types of consolidation should be tested as well. One possibility would be to establish grades 1-3 in every parish in a special building also serving as an adult education center, to which the sisters could daily commute from a central residence. Grades 4-6 and grades 7-9 could be centralized at various locations. The necessary expenditures involved in providing bus service for all students would be minuscule when compared with the financial advantage gained by avoiding duplication of resources and the academic benefits of concentration of facilities. It would also be possible to consider forming a number of school complexes with grades 1-12 located on campus-like facilities at two or three easily accessible locations within a diocese.[16]

4. *The use of the parochial school as an adult education center with a special faculty offering courses in Bible study, child psychology, and similar subjects, for all the members of the community, parishioners and non-parishioners.* In this manner increased impetus would be given to the process by which

15. Cf. Anthony E. Seidl, "Those Expensive Lay Teachers," *Commonweal*, April 23, 1965. Professor Seidl contends that the diffusion of religious salaries into various forms of compensation (convent maintenance, motherhouse contributions, etc.) and the inadequate accounting systems prevalent in Catholic schools and parishes tend to obscure the fact that the *total* cost of maintaining a salaried religious may be greater than the corresponding cost of a lay teacher.

16. For an account of the achievement of one such educational complex, see the report on the South Florida Education Center of Broward County, Fla., in *U. S. News and World Report,* July 5, 1965.

child-centered parishes could mature into adult-centered communities.[17]

> The Church is bound as a mother to give to these children of hers an education by which their whole life can be imbued with the spirit of Christ and at the same time do all she can to promote for all peoples the complete perfection of the human person, the good of earthly society and the building of a world that is more human (DCE 3).

An adult education center utilizing the school building would have unique advantages in under-privileged areas where remedial classes and special tutoring projects could be offered to potential school drop-outs along with job training courses offered to the community at large.

> Though primary and secondary schools, the foundation of education, must still be fostered, great importance is to be attached to those which are required in a particular way by contemporary conditions, such as: professional and technical schools, centers for educating adults and promoting social welfare, or for the retarded in need of special care (DCE 8).

5. *The decision to make the resources of Catholic education available to the public school program.* The Elementary and Secondary Education Act of 1965 views private and public education as partners in a common enterprise. Parochial schools will benefit from the concept of shared services which will make available materials and teachers on an interchangeable basis among the various schools within a community. The use of library and scientific material will be especially beneficial to parochial schools. Will we respond by offering the services of

17. Father Daniel A. Lord, S.J., devoted all his life to youth, but two years before he died of cancer he said publicly, "If I had my life to live over again I would work with adults. It is grown-ups who run the world, create the community climate of self-discipline or laxity which is the predominant influence in young lives"—Meyer, *The Whole World Is My Neighbor,* p. 151.

our best personnel to enrichment programs outside our own system? And will we expand our previous commitment to summer head start programs by including year-round educational projects in culturally deprived neighborhoods, thereby making a substantial contribution to public education where it is most needed?

> They [the children] should be so trained to take their part in social life that properly instructed in the necessary and opportune skills they can become actively involved in various community organizations, open to discourse with others and willing to do their best to promote the common good (DCE 1).

What will research reveal regarding the past and present efforts of the Catholic school system? Only time and the willingness to invest in research can offer an adequate answer to a question that must be answered if we are to invest our immense resources intelligently in the era of Vatican II. But it would seem reasonable to expect that a comprehensive study of the formative influences responsible for developing the men and women who successfully implemented the council in the United States will eventually reveal the schools as having been a dominant factor.

The potential effect which the schools are capable of exercising on the implementation of Vatican II is obviously immense. The past legacy of the schools was understandably centered on protective values within the Catholic community. From the Spirit speaking through the conciliar documents the schools and their personnel can now derive the inspiration to form millions with life-long commitments to the Church and to the entire community.

2. THE CONCILIAR SISTERS

It is unfortunate that the relatively small amount of publicity given to the Sister Formation Movement from its inception over a decade ago has resulted in somewhat obscuring the fact that several years prior to Pope John and Vatican II the American sisters pioneered a now remarkably successful program of self-improvement. The decisions to extend training periods and to formulate new apostolic attitudes required both enlightened judgment and considerable sacrifice on the part of the religious communities of women in the early 1950's. In many instances the sisters' determination to improve their professional status through extended and improved training prior to actual involvement in the apostolate was resisted by ecclesiastical administrators who preferred immediately available personnel rather than a necessary delay to provide more qualified religious at a later date.

Fortunately for the American Church the sisters made their program of self-help an undeniable success.[18] The goals of the Sister Formation Program (the continual development of the apostolic and professional potential of every religious through collective efforts to provide young sisters with a bachelor's degree, or its equivalent, prior to full time apostolic involvement, and to offer additional training to professed sisters as well as advanced studies for talented candidates) are being attained in increasing measure with the passage of each successive year.

So quietly have many communities executed their own program of extending and improving the training given to their members that the full significance of the change is not widely realized.[19] In many respects clergy and laity still regard these sisters as they did ten years ago, as quiet, dedicated, completely absorbed in the parish elementary school, spending a lifetime acquiring a college education through summer and Saturday

18. For a brief history of the Sister Formation Movement, see Sister Bertrande Meyers, O.C., *Sisters for the 21st Century* (New York: Sheed and Ward, 1965), pp. 104 ff.

19. For a review of apostolic programs conducted by postulants and novices, see Sister Mary Pauline, "The Direct Apostolate . . . Sisters Prepare," *Ave Maria*, March 27, 1965.

courses. But in an increasing number of cases the young sister who arrives in today's parish has already obtained her college degree (or will shortly do so), and she may even be planning for a program of graduate studies leading to an advanced degree.

Comparing her background with that of the newly ordained curate might give some indication of the dimension of the improvements. The young sister in the parish school may have had the benefit of a university milieu in her previous training, or at least she can look forward to it in her summer program; the new curate in the rectory may never have experienced a university environment, and there is small likelihood that its benefits will become available to him in his immediate future. Her future development may be carefully charted by an in-service program featuring year-round conferences on liturgical reforms and biblical advances as well as educational techniques; his future development may be a haphazard affair devoid of overall planning and dependent almost in its entirety on personal initiative.

The convent and rectory comparison of academic background would naturally vary from parish to parish and from diocese to diocese, but it should be considered when attempting to understand the growing phenomenon of tension between rectory and convent in certain parishes. In many cases a subtle (and sometimes not so subtle) difference in policy is traceable to one group's greater familiarity with the current intention and direction of the Church. In a significant number of areas the sisters are generally regarded as more responsive to the forces of renewal than the local clergy.

It was to be expected that some of the approximately 500 independent United States communities of religious women would respond rather slowly to the influence of the Sister Formation Movement. With the development of the full force of renewal in the years of Vatican II these communities inevitably became the recipients of a critical evaluation within the Church. From a distant perspective future generations may regard the criticism as a curious phenomenon. It certainly was a startling reversal of the traditional Catholic approach to the American nun which combined a reverential awe over the mystery of her life with a glorification of her past accomplishments. It was also a criticism which was generally devoid of historical perspective.

Many of the critics seemed oblivious of the fact that the practices which they so strenuously objected to were originally established by a male dominated Church which was not inclined to trust women with powers of flexibility or initiative. Also neglected in many evaluations was the fact that even today the activity pattern of the American nun remains under the general control of male dominated organizations: for example, the all-powerful Sacred Congregation for Religious, the Vatican source of rules and regulations for nuns, did not have a single woman religious involved in its work, even as a consultant. And it frequently happened that the sisters' reluctance to draw attention to clerical resistance to their own proposals for renewal resulted in popular misconceptions regarding the actual source of resistance to change.

But now that the products of the greatest development program for religious women in the history of the Church are beginning to make their presence felt in the daily life of the Church, it will not be particularly helpful to continue those banal references to supposed medievalism and hopelessly outdated characteristics. It should be obvious that the approximately 180,000 religious women in almost 500 religious orders in the United States will not be appreciably assisted by generalizations obviously inapplicable in many cases because of the wide diversity in attitude (there are liberal convents and there are conservative convents), and a similar diversity in apostolates (almost half of the United States nuns are engaged in apostolates other than school: nursing, social work, home missions, and care of the aged). It would probably be far more advantageous in advancing the cause of renewal if the faithful in each parish were to present collectively their suggestions for the specific implementation of the increasing potential of today's sister within their community.[20]

The sisters' recognized accomplishments in the development of the youngest members of the parish should not serve as a perpetual blinder to the possibility of expanding their apostolate to all parish functions.[21] It is obvious that an indispensable prerequisite to an enlarged apostolate would be the careful study and the complete removal of the many superfluous tasks now impeding an involvement of the sisters in adult work within the parish. In many (but not all) areas, the era when the nuns spent their weekends counting the parish collection, maintaining the parish sacristy, training the choir, keeping parish records and other assorted jobs has vanished into the past. But how much of the apostolic energy of today's sister is consumed in administerial and cleaning functions on school days? And how many Saturdays are devoted to small tasks which could be expeditiously handled by others? It would seem reasonable to assume that in those cases where a full-time parish secretary has proved beneficial in freeing the clergy for exclusively ministerial concerns the same service could legitimately be extended to school and convent with similar results.

The addition of salaried administration and secretarial assist-

20. "The nun, that 'high-tension Christian' (if I may use the term), ought to be able to say, 'The world is my convent.' She has no right to limit her horizon to the four walls of her school or hospital or clinic: it should extend as far as the interests of the Church"—Cardinal Suenens, *The Nun in the World,* p. 95.

21. "Once nuns are conscious of the scope of their mission and have by right assumed their place in the general pastoral picture, it is obvious that they have a place at all levels of the pastoral structure: parish councils, diocesan unions, national councils and, one day no doubt, international councils"—*Ibid.,* p. 111.

ance within the school could be expected to provide the opportunity for various commitments outside the school which would otherwise be impossible. Condolence visits to the bereaved, the sick and the aged within the parish would immediately come to mind as obvious utilizations of the kindness and the compassion characteristic of sisters. Especially gratifying to an overextended clergy would be the sisters' ability to provide personal instructions in depth for all inquirers.

Those nuns with backgrounds in liturgical or biblical studies could be expected to conduct adult education seminars in their respective fields, and it may be well to keep in mind that the nation's traditional respect for the sister would make her an ideal witness for the Church at ecumenical meetings within the neighborhood.

These suggestions for the sisters' involvement in parish life might seem somewhat overambitious to many who are personally familiar with the work load of the sisters in our elementary schools. But it is difficult to conceive of a single parish in which the possibility of several hours of adult apostolic activity for each sister every week could not be gained through some combination of alleviating factors, such as an expanded cleaning or maintenance service, the reduction of unrealistic work loads to more meaningful levels, additional clerical help, and the introduction or the more efficient use of labor-saving devices. There is not much point in quibbling over the additional capital outlay necessary to permit adult apostolic work by the sisters. It would seem that we have good reason to suspect that every year we waste a far greater sum by dissipating the efforts of expensively trained sisters on valueless minutia, and the additional expense would be fractional when compared with the vast sums now being spent in overall maintenance.

However, any attempt to initiate adult apostolic activity by the sisters within a parish depends almost entirely on the apostolic awareness of the pastor and his people. With their innate tactfulness the sisters cannot be expected to petition unilaterally for an end to their traditional isolation from activity outside the school. The religious who is overburdened with a myriad of small duties on Saturday should be able to rely on the parish's awareness of the situation that is impeding the full use of her apostolic potential. In many cases a few decisions by a pastor, combined with the agreement of the local superior, can initiate a new era of apostolic productivity in the parish. In other cases it may be necessary to petition the provincial superior for an easing of rules or customs to enable religious to work outside the school.

It is to be expected that a certain number of communities will not wish to adopt new forms of apostolic effort at this time. But it is equally to be expected that other communities will respond with enthusiasm to a pastor's request for a moderate amount of involvement outside the school, and these communities deserve to be asked. In the matter of petitions, prime attention should be given to the progressive statements currently being made by major superiors regarding their search for an increasing apostolic involvement for today's sister. Pastors and parishioners who can particularize this willingness into definite programs can be considered as enriching both their own lives and the lives of the cooperating sisters. A willingness to accept the sisters as full partners in the life of the parish may be the single, most rewarding decision a parish could make.[22]

An increasing number of opportunities for apostolic involvement would continue to suggest themselves, following the acceptance of the sisters as members of the parish family with a recog-

---

22. "We hope that they (Sisters) may get back a more direct and full participation in the life of the Church, in the liturgy in particular, in social welfare, in the modern apostolate, in the service of the brethren. A great deal is being done in this direction; and we feel that is to the benefit of the Sister's sanctification and to the benefit of the faithful who are edified" —Pope Paul VI, "New Horizons for the Woman Religious," *The Pope Speaks,* Vol. 10, No. 1, 1964.

nized potential for enriching the lives of all. The advantageous use of the various talents possessed by individual sisters could lead to an improvement of parish programs: as the selection of sisters as speakers at parish meetings, as discussion club leaders, and liturgy consultants, and would undoubtedly help to terminate the parental objection to the sisterhood as involving a loss of individual expression. The value of additional social contact between sisters and laity needs very little vindication in view of the evidence obtained by Father Fichter's study regarding the increased loyalty to the Church established in those instances in which a personal contact exists between priest and laity.

Attempts to give sisters a greater degree of participation in the life of the parish, its liturgy, its various apostolates and its service to the community may ultimately depend on how much communication can be established among the sisters and the various members of the parish community. Each sister should have the opportunity to listen to the laity and to the clergy on an individual basis, and both priest and laity must be willing to listen to the individual sister. The development of a pattern of shared authority within each convent is as beneficial to parish renewal as the formation of shared responsibility among the various members of the parish. The individual sister deserves the same hearing given to the individual priest and to the individual lay person, a willingness on the part of ecclesiastical administrators to provide lines of communication and to utilize effectively the individual's endowment of vision and initiative.

The practice of listening to the individual sister in the parish could have far-reaching consequences in the renewal of entire communities of sisters. Too many of the meetings and conferences of the Major Superiors of Religious Women are confined to the closed circles of those occupying positions of authority.[23]

23. Cf. the perceptive review by Sister Charles Borromeo, C.S.C., of *Sisters for the 21st Century* in the *National Catholic Reporter,* June 2, 1965, where she says: "The tone of extreme deference toward superiors

Dialogue within the parish could give the individual sister a ful-crum to bring the collective weight of clerical and lay opinion into the process of securing a representative sharing for each sister in the decision-making process of general chapters and major superiors.[24]

In its nuns the American Church has a unique legacy. Where else in the universal Church is the religious woman as spiritually and as intellectually prepared to become the collaborator in pastoral action, which Pope Paul VI has indicated to be the modern vocation of the sister?[25] But the utilization of this inheritance requires the cooperation of the faithful. The legacy which the sisters offer the American Church will be fully pos-

---

will irritate most of the ordinary Sisters who feel that all in a community are one in Christ and equally *are* the community. The contemporary attitude toward authority as surely great responsibility, but mainly as a ministry of service of listening and of love is already working a profound renewal in community living. To the present day, most meetings and conventions on Sisters' renewal have tended to limit discussion and decision to the closed circle of those in authority positions. . . . Those in authority usually are not involved in the actual works of their communities, and this cannot be helped perhaps. But this means that it is the voice of the ordinary Sister which alone can say how the Sisters and the community as a corporate group are affecting this slum, that school, this group of parents, these patients."

24. Sisters' Forum, a monthly feature of the *National Catholic Reporter,* is an impressive record of the dialogue among religious women. Over 7,000 individual sisters subscribe to this national Catholic newspaper.

25. "You have served in education, in the service of the sick, in schools, in hospitals. At this time the Church says, 'And now, yet more . . . become capable of doing and of giving even more. . . . I will spread you out a little, I will separate you into little groups; I will scatter you among the Christian people, who have such need of seeing the consecrated virgin in the midst of their profane society. I will put you in the very midst of society and of youth who have no other example of a life of virtue and of complete immolation. I will put you close to all my parish work. I will call you closer to my altars. I will place you in all my works for the salvation and sanctification of the world.' This is the modern vocation of the Sister—to become a collaborator in pastoral action. You have been called to become—yes, you—the Redeemer of souls, not only to cure bodies or to educate children"—Pope Paul VI, "Discourse to Sisters," quoted by Sister Gertrude Joseph Donnelly, C.S.J.O., *The Sister Apostle* (Notre Dame, Ind.: Fides, 1964), pp. 123-124.

sessed only if the Church succeeds in completely involving the sisters in the Christian life of the community.

3. CELEBRATING THE SACRAMENTS TOMORROW

A revised parish liturgy with ceremonies and symbols selected to provide maximum meaning to the participants could both indicate and intensify the parish's commitment to the neighborhood and to the world.[26] Purified of the cultural tone of an earlier age and a different environment, the liturgy could clearly reveal Christ speaking and working through the faithful in each parish in a continuous effort to bring redemption to all mankind.[27] To Christ seen in the liturgy as universally solicitous for the welfare of mankind, the faithful would respond by acting out the same concern in their daily lives. Action contributing to the welfare of the neighborhood and of the world would be understood as the indispensable preparation needed to become properly disposed for participation in the community worship.[28]

To achieve this orientation of liturgy to action it may be necessary to revise the ceremonial aspects of the sacraments.[29] The revisions would be designed to offer eminently clear manifestations of the meaning of each sacrament and to gain maxi-

26. For a discussion of the relation between liturgy and social improvement, see Robert G. Hoyt, "Liturgy and the Social Order" in Frederick R. McManus, ed., *The Revival of the Liturgy* (New York: Herder and Herder, 1963), pp. 139 ff.

27. For an analysis of the *Constitution on the Sacred Liturgy* in the light of the historical precedents and the work of the liturgical movement, see J. D. Crichton, *The Church's Worship* (New York: Sheed and Ward, 1964).

28. "Liturgy which does not move its participants to social action is mere ceremonialism; social action which does not find its source in the Liturgy is mere humanitarianism. Here is the test of true Liturgy; does it make those who participate more charitable, does it make them more conscious of their duties toward their brothers, does it make them more concerned for the needs of the community?"—Richard Cardinal Cushing of Boston, in a pastoral letter.

29. For a presentation of specific proposals in revitalizing the liturgy, see Dom Adrien Nocent, O.S.B., *The Future of the Liturgy* (New York: Herder and Herder, 1963).

mum benefit for the recipient through complete participation.

> With the passage of time, however, there have crept into the rites of the sacraments and sacramentals certain features which have rendered their nature and purpose far from clear to the people of today; hence some changes have become necessary to adapt them to the needs of our own times (CSL 62).

> For the liturgy is made up of immutable elements divinely instituted, and of elements subject to change. These not only may but ought to be changed with the passage of time if they have suffered from the intrusion of anything out of harmony with the inner nature of the liturgy or have become unsuited to it.

> In this restoration, both texts and rites should be drawn up so that they express more clearly the holy things which they signify; the Christian people, so far as possible, should be enabled to understand them with ease and to take part in them fully, actively, and as befits a community (CSL 21).

Various forms of adaptation are possible.

Baptism. The sacrament of initiation could be revised to permit the use of a ceremony with a format common to many Christian Churches, thus making clear to all Christians the common bond which they share in Christ. The baptism of children could become an integral part of a particular Mass each Sunday morning in which a large part of the parish community would share the joy of parents and reflect the happiness of the entire parish in the conferral of Christ's life. The baptism of adults would occur during the Easter vigil ceremony and would be preceded by successive steps of entry into the Christian community at periodic intervals during Lent. In this manner the entire community could more fully appreciate the significance of the saving act of incorporation into God's people.

> The catechumenate for adults, comprising several distinct steps, is to be restored and to be taken into use at the dis-

cretion of the local ordinary. By this means the time of the catechumenate, which is intended as a period of suitable instruction, may be sanctified by sacred rites to be celebrated at successive intervals of time (CSL 64).

More use is to be made of the baptismal features proper to the Lenten liturgy; some of them, which used to flourish in bygone days, are to be restored as may seem good (CSL 119).

Confirmation. Vatican II has officially recognized the pastor's role in the administration of this sacrament in the Eastern Churches.

The established practice in respect of the minister of confirmation that has obtained from most early times in the Eastern Church should be fully restored. Therefore, priests validly confer this sacrament, using chrism blessed by a patriarch or a bishop (DCC 13).

Conferral of the sacrament of confirmation by the pastor in United States parishes would seem to have a number of advantages. The meaning of the sacrament as the acceptance of a personal commitment in Christ to the community and to the world would be more evident if it were administered by the pastor as the presiding official within the local community to young people at the dawn of maturity, or approximately sixteen years of age. A revised ceremony within the framework of a special Mass would show the sacrament's close relationship to the Christian initiation begun at baptism and shared in by the entire community. As part of the ceremony the recipients could make a pledge to Christian commitment within their own parish and to any other area as determined by the Church's needs.

The rite of confirmation is to be revised and the intimate connection which this sacrament has with the whole of Christian initiation is to be more clearly set forth; for this reason it is fitting for candidates to renew their baptismal promises just before they are confirmed.

Confirmation may be given within the Mass when convenient; when it is given outside the Mass, the rite that is to be used should be introduced by a formula to be drawn up for this purpose (CSL 71).

They are more perfectly bound to the Church by the sacrament of confirmation, and the Holy Spirit endows them with special strength so that they are more strictly obliged to spread and defend the faith, both by word and by deed, as true witnesses of Christ (CC 11).

The Holy Eucharist. Self-administered and in a form and quantity sufficient to indicate its nature as food, the Eucharist would be clearly seen to be the product of a common table through which the Father unites each Christian with his Son and with one another. The privilege of bearing the Eucharist to the sick within the parish or in hospitals could be conferred upon family members of the sick as an indication of their unity in Christ.

They should give thanks to God; by offering the immaculate victim, not only through the hands of the priests, but also with him, they should learn also to offer themselves; through Christ the Mediator, they should be drawn day by day into ever more perfect union with God and with each other, so that finally God may be all in all (CSL 48).

Penance. In a special ceremony composed of penitential readings from the Bible and congregational expression of sorrow over common faults and failings, there would be revealed both the personal nature of sin and the social consequences of sin within this community. Before the individual reception of the sacrament of penance the entire congregation would request forgiveness from both God and from one another, and make mutual pledges of repentance and improvement.

The rite and formulas for the sacrament of penance are to be revised so that they more clearly express both the nature and effect of the sacrament (CSL 72).

Those who approach the sacrament of penance obtain pardon from the mercy of God for the offence committed against Him and are at the same time reconciled with the Church, which they have wounded by their sins, and which by charity, example, and prayer seeks their conversion (CC 11).

Holy Orders and Profession of Vows. The true nature of the sacrament of ordination as both a divine endowment and the symbolic manifestation of the bestowal of the grace of service would be clear by conferring the sacrament in its various forms (the minor offices of reader and exorcist, etc., the major offices of deacon and deaconess) upon the men and women of the parish by the bishop and the pastor acting together. Once a year there would be an annual renewal of these commitments in a special ceremony, renewing the original commitment made through the Spirit for the purpose of enriching the entire community.

It is the Holy Spirit, dwelling in those who believe and pervading and ruling over the entire Church, who brings about that wonderful communion of the faithful and joins them together so intimately in Christ that He is the principle of the Church's unity. By distributing various kinds of spiritual gifts and ministries, He enriches the Church of Jesus Christ with different functions "in order to equip the saints for the work of service, so as to build up the body of Christ" Eph 4:12 (DOE 2).

Matrimony. The sacrament would be administered Sunday morning or afternoon during a community Mass as the celebration of the entire parish whose unity is intensified by each bond in Christ. The ceremony would be enriched by additional scripture readings referring to marital love and its contribution to the community.

The marriage rite now found in the Roman Ritual is to be revised and enriched in such a way that the grace of the sacrament is more clearly signified and the duties of the spouses are taught (CSL 77).

The Anointing of the Sick. During Sunday morning Mass the entire Christian community would participate in the administration of this sacrament to those of its members who because of any illness would need both the saving power of the sacrament and the accompanying display of unity on the part of those in attendance. At the conclusion of Mass a special group of the faithful could be delegated to go to the home of anyone too sick to be present, in order to represent the parish in the conferral of the sacrament.

> "Extreme unction," which may also and more fittingly be called "anointing of the sick," is not a sacrament for those only who are at the point of death. Hence, as soon as any one of the faithful begins to be in danger of death from sickness or old age, the fitting time for him to receive this sacrament has certainly already arrived (CSL 73).

> By the sacred anointing of the sick and the prayer of her priests the whole Church commends the sick to the suffering and glorified Lord, asking that He may lighten their suffering and save them; she exhorts them, moreover, to contribute to the welfare of the whole people of God by associating themselves freely with the passion and death of Christ (CC 11).

The Decree on the Catholic Churches of the Eastern Rite recognizes the value of a certain sharing of the sacraments among Christians.

> Pastoral experience shows clearly that, as regards our Eastern brethren, there should be taken into consideration the different cases of individuals, where neither the unity of the Church is hurt nor are verified the dangers that must be avoided, but where the needs of the salvation of souls and their spiritual good are impelling motives. For that reason the Catholic Church has always adopted and now adopts rather a mild policy, offering to all the means of salvation and an example of charity among Christians, through participation in the sacraments and in other sacred functions and things (DCC 26).

It would seem reasonable to expect that among Protestant Christians there would also be many "separated in good faith" who under certain conditions could be admitted to the sacraments. The problem is complex and it would be difficult to formulate a general policy, but perhaps individual cases may be admitted on the basis of varying circumstances.

4. TOMORROW'S MASS

It will be essential that the true nature of the parish and its commitment to neighborhood, community and world be clearly evident through its joyous celebration of the Lord's banquet. Celebrated on different days in different places within the parish (apartments, private homes, and places of work) the Mass would encourage encounter with Christ and with fellow Christians in the actual scenes of daily life. The structure of the Mass could be modified into a format capable of demonstrating clearly its meaning to contemporary man.

> The rite of the Mass is to be revised in such a way that the intrinsic nature and purpose of its several parts, as also the connection between them, may be more clearly manifested, and that devout and active participation by the faithful may be more easily achieved.
>
> For this purpose the rites are to be simplified, due care being taken to preserve their substance; elements which, with the passage of time, came to be duplicated, or were added with but little advantage, are now to be discarded; other elements which have suffered injury through accidents of history are now to be restored to the vigor which they had in the days of the holy Fathers, as may seem useful or necessary (CSL 50).

A revised structure might include the following elements:

1. By a procession involving the entire congregation, or at least a representative number on a rotating basis, the faithful would express and experience their unity with one another. Through its music the community would indicate collectively

the basic joyfulness of a banquet to which all have been invited by the Lord himself. The *Constitution on the Sacred Liturgy* has established the general principle that the music of the sacred liturgy is to be adapted to the general pattern of music in certain parts of the world.

> In certain parts of the world, especially mission lands, there are peoples who have their own musical traditions, and these play a great part in their religious and social life. For this reason due importance is to be attached to their music, and a suitable place is to be given to it, not only in forming their attitude towards religion, but also in adapting worship to their native genius, as indicated in Art. 39 and 40 (CSL 119).

The expected extension of this principle of musical adaptation to the entire world seems to be foreshadowed in the constitution's recognition of the possibility of a variety of instruments in sacred worship.

> In the Latin Church the pipe organ is to be held in high esteem, . . . But other instruments also may be admitted for use in divine worship, with the knowledge and consent of the competent territorial authority (CLS 120).

The acceptance of the music of a nation in its liturgy would seem to be an integral part of the adaptation of worship to culture.

2. The ornate formalism of the ancient orations could be amended by a spontaneous form of prayer using daily language and common images from everyday life. Frequently, the prayer could be prepared by the congregation itself.

3. The lessons would include several readings from the Old and New Testaments and would be based on an extensive cycle of Bible readings shared by many Christian communities on the same day. In this way the entire Bible could be read and considered over a period of years and Christians attending one another's Churches would realize their common legacy.

The treasures of the Bible are to be opened up more lav-
ishly, so that richer fare may be provided for the faithful at
the table of God's word. In this way a more representative
portion of the holy scriptures will be read to the people in
the course of a prescribed number of years (CSL 51).

4. The homily should be a proclamation of God's saving
message as found in the Sacred Scriptures, and the community's
response to this message here and now.

The sermon, moreover, should draw its content mainly
from scriptural and liturgical sources, and its character
should be that of a proclamation of God's wonderful works
in the history of salvation, the mystery of Christ, ever made
present and active within us, especially in the celebration of
the liturgy (CSL 34).

There could also be a sharing of the preaching office among
priests, deacons and lay members of the congregation. At certain
times a group discussion might constitute the concluding part of
the homily. Parishioners interested in a further development of
the implications of the homily could be guests at a coffee session
after Mass.

5. In addition to the regularly formulated petitions of the
community, the prayer of the faithful would consist of periods
of silent petition following the expressed intentions of those
members of the community who wished to solicit the prayers of
all.

6. Through a wide variety of gifts symbolic of the community's daily activity and aspirations, carried to the altar by a
procession representative of the entire congregation, there would
be made clear the collective nature of the community's action at
the offertory of the Mass. A simplified offertory rite could dis-
pense with many of the verbal redundancies characteristic of the
present ceremony and would bring this part of the Mass closer
to the desired norm.

The rites should be distinguished by a noble simplicity;

they should be short, clear, and unencumbered by useless repetitions; they should be within the people's powers of comprehension, and normally should not require much explanation (CSL 34).

7. A revised canon, prayed in the vernacular by all present, either in unison or in alternating parts, would be unmistakably a prayer of thanksgiving in which all participate. A greater amount of seasonal variation in its content would reduce the formalism of its current expression.

8. The Eucharist, self-administered and received simultaneously in a form symbolic of its nature as food, would be seen clearly as the life-giving sustenance of the faithful.

9. The Mass would conclude with an assignment to the execution of some aspects of its message. The final blessing would be accompanied by a pledge of the faithful to a particular program bringing spiritual or social enrichment to the community, for example, participation in a program of religious formation or a neighborhood improvement project.

Christ's redemptive work, while essentially concerned with the salvation of men, includes also the renewal of the whole temporal order. Hence the mission of the Church is not only to bring the message and grace of Christ to men but also to penetrate and perfect the temporal order with the spirit of the Gospel (DOL 5).

The adaptation of the liturgy to local needs will require a variety of attempts to determine the particular methods most effective in making God's redemptive act present and readily perceivable within the complex environment of modern life.

To ensure that adaptations may be made with all the circumspection which they demand, the Apostolic See will grant power to this same territorial ecclesiastical authority to permit and to direct, as the case requires, the necessary preliminary experiments over a determined period of time among certain groups suited for the purpose (CSL 40).

The rite for the burial of the dead is one example of a particular ceremony that will require considerable experimentation. The task is to determine the most suitable method of relating each Christian's death to the saving act of Christ's death and resurrection. The present rite with its heavily penitential overtones is hardly reflective of the joyful result of Christ's redemptive work.

> The rite for the burial of the dead should express more clearly the paschal character of Christian death, and should correspond more closely to the circumstances and traditions found in various regions. This holds good also for the liturgical color to be used (CSL 81).

The use of biblical texts and prayers stressing the enduring association of Christ with Christians in the paschal event of death and resurrection, as well as the liturgical expression of collective joy over another resurrection, would assist in the process of recovering the kerygmatic concept of Christ as the destroyer of the death which the world fears. Other forms of worship will also require experimentation, especially Bible services, which can be expected to become an accepted part of Christian worship in homes and apartments where the people of God must exercise their own priesthood.

> Bible services should be encouraged . . . where no priest is available; when this is so, a deacon or some other person authorized by the bishop should preside over the celebration (CSL 35.4).

5. UNITY ON THE GROUND FLOOR

One of the most encouraging phenomena of the post-Vatican II world is the series of high level efforts aimed at developing Christian unity. A series of multi-lateral theological discussions with Lutherans, Episcopalians, Presbyterians and Orthodox have been established by the bishops' Commission for Ecumenical Affairs. The American bishops have also framed guidelines for inter-confessional activity, and during the annual Church

Unity Week many dioceses sponsor inter-confessional liturgical services to pray for unity. The majority of dioceses have appointed ecumenical commissions to encourage and direct ecumenical efforts officially.

Yet there is evidence to indicate that the ecumenical movement has not made a significant impact on the life of the average congregation. In a poll conducted by the *Christian Herald,* 85 percent of the participants believed that unity among Protestants and Catholics would be undesirable. Ministers and priests engaged in ecumenical activity on the congregational level have indicated that official statements made by Church leaders do not always reflect a consensus of thought among their membership. Thus it would seem that an immediate need of the ecumenical movement is a broadening of its grass roots support.

It is significant that the council's *Decree on Ecumenism* does not indicate that ecumenical activities are to be confined to those occupying predominant positions in the Church. Instead the council fathers encourage effort by every member of the people of God.

> Today, in many parts of the world, under the inspiring grace of the Holy Spirit, many efforts are being made in prayer, word and action to attain that fullness of unity which Jesus Christ desires. The sacred Council exhorts, therefore, all the Catholic faithful to recognize the signs of the times and to take an active and intelligent part in the work of ecumenism (DOE 4).

A good case could be made for the belief that efforts toward unity will either live or die depending on what individual Christians decide to do in individual congregations. These decisions could be considered as occurring in stages.

Needless to say ecumenical efforts will not be initiated by parishes unless the members are convinced that unity among Christians is desirable. In many instances it will be necessary to re-evaluate former opinions and views. The earlier years of isolation among Churches, and the resulting impression of self-sufficiency, may constitute a formidable impediment to a community's full realization that disunity among Christians is a scandal.

> Many Christian Communions present themselves to men as the true inheritors of Jesus Christ; all indeed profess to be followers of the Lord but they differ in mind and go their different ways, as if Christ Himself were divided. Certainly, such division openly contradicts the will of Christ, scandalizes the world, and damages that most holy cause, the preaching of the Gospel to every creature (DOE 1).

Are we really convinced that it is God's will that each Christian work for unity?

> The concern for restoring unity involves the whole Church, faithful and clergy alike. It extends to everyone, according to the talent of each, whether it be exercised in daily Christian living or in theological and historical studies (DOE 5).

And are we certain that we have much to gain through an interchange of patterns of worship, religious insights, and so forth?

> Nor should we forget that anything wrought by the grace of the Holy Spirit in the hearts of our separated brethren can contribute to our own edification. Whatever is truly Christian is never contary to what genuinely belongs to the faith; indeed, it can always bring a more perfect realization of the very mystery of Christ and the Church (DOE 4).

Since the process of achieving unity will require a considerable expenditure of energy and time, it is important that efforts in this direction be derived from firm convictions among Christians that it is God's will that they devote perhaps a lifetime of effort to the cause of uniting all the brothers of Christ in the one family desired by our common Father.[30]

30. "Mutual understanding among the Churches is going to demand a great many adaptations. These, beyond any question, will transform both men and organizations, but it will be at a slow and measured pace, a pace

The decision to enter into serious and comprehensive discussions of religious differences on the parish level could be considered as the second stage in ecumenical endeavor. Dialogues among members of the various Christian communities within their respective homes are generally regarded as offering the best environment for an open and friendly discussion of religious differences.

> Most valuable for this purpose are meetings of the two sides—especially for discussion of theological problems— where each can treat with the other on an equal footing, provided that those who take part in them under the guidance of the authorities are truly competent. From such dialogue will emerge still more clearly what the situation of the Catholic Church really is. In this way, too, we will better understand the outlook of our separated brethren and more aptly present our own belief (DOE 9).

A comparison of religious beliefs and attitudes on a social basis can be expected to do more than help to form a Christian solidarity: the resulting dialogue will also lead individual Protestants and Catholics to learn their own faith with a degree of insight which they may never have experienced previously. But the various programs will be successful only if they are carefully planned. The *Living Room Dialogues* developed by the National Council of Churches and the Catholic Confraternity of Christian Doctrine Program offer one line of possible development. Other patterns of discussion may be developed on a limited scale by experimental groups and then made available for wider use within a particular area.[31]

---

which will sometimes be uncertain. If it is extremely difficult to arouse the entire Christian people to a consciousness of being 'in state of mission,' it is going to be every bit as arduous to involve the entire Church in an 'ecumenical age' "—Cardinal Suenens, *The Church in Dialogue*, pp. 26-27.

31. See also *An Evening of Christian Friendship*, a booklet based on the inter-faith program developed by the Worcester Council of Churches and the Confraternity of Christian Doctrine of the Diocese of Worcester.

The prayer service in which Pope Paul participated with Orthodox, Anglican and Protestant observers at the conclusion of Vatican II was both a precedent and a guide to future ecumenical prayer. The service was neither distinctly Catholic nor Protestant; it was a mutual act of common worship based on biblical reading and congregational response.

> In certain special circumstances, such as in prayer services "for unity" and during ecumenical gatherings, it is allowable, indeed desirable that Catholics should join in prayer with their separated brethren. Such prayers in common are certainly a very effective means of petitioning for the grace of unity, and they are a genuine expression of the ties which still bind Catholics to their separated brethren. "For where two or three are gathered together in my name, there am I in the midst of them" Mt 18:20 (DOE 8).

The ecumenical guidelines subsequently established by the United States Bishops' Commission for Ecumenical Affairs offer United States bishops offer a broad range of possibilities.

> With the approval of the local bishop, priests are to be encouraged to take an active part in the conduct of [ecumenical] services, e.g., by reading Scripture lessons, preaching, homilies, offering prayers and giving blessings. . . . On occasion, members of the Catholic laity may also be invited to take an active part in ecumenical services. They may, for example, be called upon to read the Scripture lessons. Under the guidance of the local bishop, who may well wish to consult his ecumenical commission regarding the qualifications of the laity invited to take these leading roles, such participation on the part of laymen has much to recommend it. *Interim Guidelines of the U. S. Bishops' Commission for Ecumenical Affairs.*[32]

32. "In accordance with Section 8 of the *Decree on Ecumenism* the participation of Catholics with other Christians in services that are not part of the official liturgies of any communion is highly desirable, providing these services are devoted to the cause of Christian unity. Such services could fittingly be called 'ecumenical services.'

"With the approval of the local bishop, priests are to be encouraged to take an active part in the conduct of services, e.g., by reading Scripture

Christians praying for Church unity according to the pattern of the special brochure co-sponsored by the American bishops, the National Council of Churches and the World Council of Churches are both an encouragement and an inspiration to one another on the long road to unity.

The use of common prayer books, the adoption of identical biblical lessons on the same Sundays and the development of a common formula for such ceremonies as baptism and marriage are additional gains in establishing unity among brethren. The development of a common ritual of ceremonies will require collaboration among Church leaders which will be productive only if Christians, by reason of their experiences of common prayer, are prepared to accept further developments. Without a frequent encounter in common prayer it is possible that ecumenical efforts could become a purely academic matter with only a slight impact on the daily lives of Christians. But with a pattern of shared prayer experiences in one another's Churches, Christians can develop the attitude and the programs leading to ever closer bonds among Churches.

The decision to discuss together and to pray together should be re-enforced by a decision to be committed together.

> Cooperation among Christians vividly expresses that bond which already unites them, and it sets in clear relief the features of Christ the Servant. . . . It should also be inten-

---

lessons, preaching homilies, offering prayers and giving blessings.

"On occasion, members of the Catholic laity may also be invited to take an active part in ecumenical services. They may, for example, be called upon to read the Scripture lessons. Under the guidance of the local bishop, who may well wish to consult his ecumenical commission regarding the qualifications of the laity invited to take these leading roles, such participation on the part of laymen has much to recommend it. The acceptance of such a policy could become one more manifestation of the Church's doctrine on the laity as found in the *Constitution on the Church*"—"Interim Guidelines for Prayer in Common and *Communicatio in Sacris*," released June 18, 1965 by the U. S. Bishops' Commission for Ecumenical Affairs, reprinted in *Catholic Mind,* Oct., 1965.

sified in the use of every possible means to relieve the afflictions of our times, such as famine and natural disasters, illiteracy and poverty, lack of housing, and the unequal distribution of wealth. Through such cooperation, all believers in Christ are able to learn easily how they can understand each other better and esteem each other more, and how the road to the unity of Christians may be made smooth (DOE 12).

The Christian impact upon the general community will be really effective only when Christians can speak with the same voice and act with the same hands to make Christ present in the community through their united manifestation of his love. This manifestation may take various forms, depending on the particular locale, but generally speaking the immediate Christian commitment will be to the underprivileged, the afflicted, and the victims of discrimination. Perhaps the greatest boost to ecumenical efforts will occur when the different Churches become convinced that their various efforts at community improvement—cooperative housing, credit unions, special job training institutes, community improvement centers, family welfare organizations, youth centers—should always be joint efforts under their collective direction.

Each step toward unity will make the next step easier. Each step will also be progressively more beneficial to all concerned. Catholics can be expected to benefit from Protestant emphasis on a biblical spirituality and the common priesthood of all believers[33]; Protestants may derive similar benefits from the liturgical emphasis and the sacramental nature of Catholicism. The day of final unity may be in the distant future, but the converging steps should be daily steps.

33. *Voices of Our Brothers,* a bi-weekly newsletter edited by Dale Francis, offers summaries of important articles appearing in over a hundred Protestant publications. It also covers significant religious material from Orthodox publications, Jewish magazines and newspapers as well as the secular press.

The result will be that, little by little, as the obstacles to perfect ecclesiastical communion are overcome, all Christians will be gathered, in a common celebration of the Eucharist, into the unity of the one and only Church, which Christ bestowed on His Church from the beginning (DOE 4).

6. THE NEW EVERYBODY

What will be the future development of the American parish? It seems likely that the parish-centered organizations of the past will be supplemented by community-centered organizations, while individual efforts at self-sanctification will be augmented by collective efforts towards the sanctification of the community.[34]

Tomorrow's parish will hopefully be a community with a commitment to the neighborhood and to the world. The commitment to the neighborhood may take various forms. It could mean combined efforts with other local Churches in joint programs designed for the spiritual enrichment of all. It could also mean participation with other Churches in municipally endowed programs of social improvement.[35]

But the commitment of the parish will extend beyond its presently conceived geographical borders. The motivation for this extension will be the realization that the local Church is Christ carrying out his redemptive work for all with whom his members come into contact.[36] The feudal concept of a geographical parish will be somewhat modified by a return to the group pattern of Christian penetration of an entire area by teams or groups having a shared responsibility of vast extent.[37] Today's

34. For a consideration of the various forms which future parish life may assume, see "The Parish—1980" by the editors of *Commonweal*, March 25, 1966.

35. See George D. Younger, *The Church and Urban Renewal* (New York: Lippincott, 1965). Pastor Younger sees a vital role in urban renewal for the local parish whose members should stand up and ask human questions of the planners and the renewers.

36. See "The Theology of the Parish," an address given by John Quinlan at the 1965 Liturgical Week, Baltimore, Md.

37. "Thus, from the very beginning, besides the ideal episcopal com-

geographical parish will continue to have value because of its undeniable advantage of establishing a point of unity, bringing together the wide variety of gifts and talents of individuals.[38] But the commitment of those united in a parish will be as extensive as their range of movement within society.

The penetration of the area beyond the strict confines of the parish may see the laity forming specialized ministry teams which will operate missions at factories and in business establishments, utilizing the technique of group encounters to discuss the Word and its specific implementation in that locale. Special ministry teams composed of Protestant, Orthodox and Catholic members may constitute a joint mission to an inner-city area, bringing their skills and resources with the Christian message.

> Let the layman not imagine that his pastors are always such experts that to every problem which arises, however complicated, they can readily give him a concrete solution, or even that such is their mission. Rather, enlightened by Christian wisdom and giving close attention to the teaching authority of the Church, let the layman take on his own distinctive role (PCC 43).

The commitment of the parish may extend considerably

---

munity, there was a graduated distribution of the full episcopal powers among several persons working closely with the bishop. With this hierarchical structure there was linked a feeling for the principle of subsidiarity which allowed each member to fulfil its function. The isolated cleric was rather exceptional, his state was due to missionary exigencies. Normally the clergy formed a community.

"In short, the parish organization goes back both to the presbyter-communities which developed into episcopal communities and to those that reverted from episcopal status. While the episcopal communities were the starting-point or the goal, the forerunners of the parish are in a state of flux, no self-contained whole but always related to the episcopal community"—Blochlinger, *The Modern Parish Community*, p. 50.

38. For an account of the remarkable record of the inner-city program of Saints Paul and Augustine Parish, Washington, D. C., see Geno Baroni, "The Church and the War on Poverty," *American Ecclesiastical Review*, September, 1965.

farther. It is conceivable that many parishes could organize and finance special teams of laity which would collectively volunteer for a limited term of annual service in a parish somewhere else in the world.[39]

> Those Christians are to be praised and supported, therefore, who volunteer their services to help other men and nations. Indeed, it is the duty of the whole People of God, following the word and example of the bishops, to alleviate as far as they are able the sufferings of the modern age (PCC 88).

7. WHICH WAY THE U.S.A.?

The American parish has an impressive number of natural endowments to use in responding to the intention of the Spirit as presented in Vatican II. Practices of harmonious discussion and parliamentary procedure common in community affairs, plus habits of delegation and sincere acceptance of commitments, provide both the inclination and the skill necessary to make the conciliar ideal of shared responsibility a reality in the daily lives of Christians.

> The Church fosters and takes to itself, insofar as they are good, the ability, riches and customs in which the genius of each people expresses itself. Taking them to itself it purifies, strengthens, elevates and enobles them (CC 13).

A healthy pride in their past accomplishments and an optimistic belief in the collective power of united action are also present with sufficient intensity among clergy and laity to arouse great expectations for the future. Whether these expectations are realized will ultimately depend on what individuals do in individual parishes.

39. E.g., All Saints Parish in Houston has a sister-parish relationship of assistance to Todos Santon (All Saints) Parish in Huehuetenango, Guatemala. See Robert S. Maxwell, M.M., "What One Diocese Can Do," *Maryknoll*, April, 1965.

Chapter Four

THE CHURCH IN THE NATION:
UNITED FOR GREATNESS

Historians of Vatican II may some day regard October 12, 1962, as a day of major importance in the modern history of the Church. On that day the bishops, under the impetus supplied by the French and German hierarchies, insisted on a recess in the council so that regional and national groups of bishops could independently meet to consider possible nominations to the commissions directing its work.

This event served as an important precedent in establishing a pattern of smaller, regional meetings of bishops during the council to prepare either a group consideration or a collective response to matters being discussed in the general assembly. The adoption of this practice may prove to be most consequential for the future life of the Church. Those familiar with the intricacies of Church machinery have long realized that the success of any attempt to achieve an initiative-producing decentralization of ecclesiastical authority in the post-conciliar world will not depend primarily on a reduction in power of the curia or central bureaucracy of the Church, although this remains an urgent necessity. Instead the key factor in establishing habits of flexible response and initiative within the Church will be whether or not the various national and international conferences of bishops have sufficient freedom of decision to balance the element of inflexibility inevitably present in any form of over-centralized control.

Prior to Vatican II there were approximately forty national or international conferences of bishops. These were not entrusted by Rome with any binding authority, but were permitted to exercise varying degrees of initiative.[1] A few national conferences, as those of the French and German hierarchies, had a tradition of deciding policy apart from any supervision by the apostolic delegate or the nuncio to their respective countries. Other episcopal conferences operated under either the chairmanship of the bishop selected by the Vatican or the constant surveillance of an apostolic delegate, and these conferences understandably had less freedom. The American Episcopal Conference, which had been in existence in one form or another for almost half a century, had never made a nationwide decision prior to Vatican II. Its exhortations could either be observed or neglected by the respective bishops in their own dioceses.

The American tradition of episcopal "rugged individualism" was evident at Vatican II. Other national hierarchies met frequently to bring their collective wisdom and influence to bear on particular issues. In contrast, many American bishops pursued individual courses of action which in a massive assembly of the size of Vatican II proved less capable of exercising the necessary leverage on the council. Some idea of the potential contribution of strong episcopal conferences to the life of the Church may be gained from recalling that it was the French and German hierarchies which arrived at the council in the best state of preparedness, and that it was these same hierarchies which made highly successful (and possibly council-saving) interventions in the early stages of Vatican II.

1. For a brief history of episcopal conferences, see Piet Fransen, S.J., "Episcopal Conferences: Crucial Problem of the Council," *Ecumenism and Vatican II*, edited by Charles O'Neill, S.J. (Milwaukee: Bruce, 1964).

1. VATICAN II AND THE NATIONAL HIERARCHIES

A very consequential aftermath of the *Constitution on the Sacred Liturgy* was the power vested for the first time in the national conferences of bishops to make binding decisions in liturgical matters upon their own members by a two-thirds vote. This concession was obviously made to avoid the liturgical anarchy within a nation which would probably have occurred under the customary system of permitting an individual bishop to make whatever exceptions he desired in the general norms adopted by his fellow bishops. But this grant of limited power did constitute a democratic advance in ecclesiastical structure by its removal of some decisionary power from the curial bureaucracy in Rome, and by its establishment of the principle of majority rule on the part of those most competent to decide on matters requiring a national policy.

Vatican II subsequently adopted a policy officially permitting the bishops of a nation—or episcopal conferences, as they are technically referred to, since different nations may combine to form a single conference—to exercise a predominant role over Church affairs within their own membership.

> An episcopal conference is, as it were, a council in which the bishops of a given nation or territory jointly exercise their pastoral office to promote the greater good which the Church offers mankind, especially through the forms and methods of the apostolate fittingly adapted to the circumstances of the age (DCP 38).

> Episcopal conferences—already established in many nations —have furnished outstanding proofs of a more fruitful apostolate. Therefore, this sacred synod considers it to be supremely fitting that everywhere bishops belonging to the same nation or region form an association which would meet at fixed times. Thus, when the insights of prudence and experience have been shared and views exchanged, there will emerge a holy union of energies in the service of the common good of the Churches (DCP 37).

Of course the crucial decision involved how much power was to be given to the conferences, and what procedure was to be followed in the decision-making process within the conference. Although the actual grant of power was carefully hedged by being confined to matters to be determined by central authority, the same basic procedure adopted earlier in the case of liturgical decisions became the regular norm.

> Decisions of the episcopal conference, provided they have been approved legitimately and by the votes of at least two-thirds of the prelates who have a deliberative vote in the conference, and have been recognized by the Apostolic See, are to have juridically binding force only in those cases prescribed by the common law or determined by a special mandate of the Apostolic See, given either spontaneously or in response to a petition of the conference itself (DCP 38 [4]).

Thus the bishops of the United States and the entire faithful now have the opportunity to adapt Church life to the American situation through the power of collective decisions in matters previously reserved to the competency of the various offices of the Roman curia. This brings us to the central question of this chapter.

2. DISCOVERING THE WISDOM OF THE FAITHFUL

What process will the American bishops use to discover the collective wisdom of the faithful prior to a joint episcopal decision? Will the pre-Vatican II practice of confining discussion to a closed episcopal meeting be adequate in the post-Vatican II era? Or should there be some means devised whereby the new episcopal power to decide on nation-wide commitments could be prefaced with a discussion that would allow the collective nation-wide wisdom of the faithful to enlighten and assist the episcopacy?

Once again the procedure followed by the Second Vatican

Council in its deliberations may be helpful in considering the pattern of conciliar implementation. In the later sessions of the council a limited number of laity were selected to assist the commissions preparing the conciliar documents, and several lay speakers had the opportunity to address the assembly. This practice represented a valuable development supplementing the earlier pattern of informal consultation among the bishops and those laity who happened to be in Rome in various capacities. The further development of opportunities for direct involvement of lay representatives in the decision-making apparatus of the Church deserves careful consideration if the conciliar ideal of shared responsibility is to be realized in the post-Vatican II era.

Could the development of lay involvement in the American Church be advanced by holding a bi-annual national synod or assembly of diocesan delegates, clerical and lay, under the joint presidency of the entire episcopate?[2] The assembly might follow the general procedure of the Vatican Council: commissions elected by the assembly could prepare position papers on the various problems confronting the Church which could then become subject matter for open discussion. The entire American Church would be represented by clerical and lay delegates elected by the respective diocesan assemblies. The decisions of the assembly would be subject to final ratification by the nation's bishops, who could alternately preside and participate in a manner similar to the episcopal presidents of Vatican II.[3]

2. "The participation of the laity was regarded as an essential feature of great councils from the Lateran in 1215 to Trent, inclusive, when they became essentially councils for reform and, more generally, councils of Christendom, assemblies to ensure unanimity—and so effectiveness—for decisions concerning crusades, the peace of the Christian commonwealth, or some work for the wellbeing of the Church. The widest possible representation of the different 'estates' and corporations, of the chief sovereign or feudal powers, seemed at that time to be essential to a council and its oecumenicity"—Yves M.-J. Congar, O.P., *Lay People in the Church*, p. 237.

3. In a joint pastoral letter read in all churches on Christmas Day, 1965, the Dutch hierarchy announced plans for a national synod to be held in 1967. Laymen will be actively involved in the meeting intended to coordi-

A representative assembly of the entire American Church would offer to the hierarchy its reflective wisdom and experience in many fields. The complexity of the nation's problems—such as race, the inner-city, poverty, ecumenical cooperation—obviously require a collective examination to determine the best means of applying the Christian message. It is difficult to imagine how the bishops can fulfill the enormous responsibility which they have for the entire American Church without some effective method of channeling the perception and the wisdom of the entire body of the faithful into a usable form.

> They [the bishops] should set forth the ways by which are to be answered the most serious questions concerning the ownership, increase, and just distribution of material goods, peace and war, and brotherly relations among all countries. . . . With a special affection they should attend upon the poor and the lower classes to whom the Lord sent them to preach the Gospel (DCP 12-13).

It is obvious that no single group within the Church will have all the answers to any complex problem, but in many cases various dioceses and committed Christians will have the beginnings of the answers. On the basis of their thoughts as representatively distilled from many sources, the entire episcopate could decide on the direction of efforts and resources within the Church during each two-year period. Delegates elected by the assembly to the various commissions would be responsible for the execution of various aspects of the assembly's program during the period between sessions. Their reports would serve as the basis for further consideration in each successive assembly.

Fundamental to a national synod is the explicit recognition that problems common to many dioceses are the problems of the

---

nate on a national level plans for implementing the decrees of Vatican II.

The Dutch hierarchy had earlier established a national pastoral institute with a predominantly lay membership concerned with relations among bishops, priests and laity, ecumenism, family problems, liturgy, etc.

entire people of God.[4] For example, a collective examination of
the dimensions of the inner-city by those competent, in an open
assembly, would do more to intensify the Christian response to
the problem than any number of moral exhortations delivered
from the top down. In certain dioceses groups of committed
Christians have pioneered efforts at racial cooperation, housing
requirements, and social action conferences. These could be
utilized by the entire Church. The transfer of their know-how to
other dioceses cannot be conducted exclusively on paper. It
requires life-giving, person-to-person contact among committed
Christians to interchange charisms effectively. An assembly of
delegates representative of the whole of every diocese in the
country could quickly effect that local implementation which
nation-wide conferences of specialized apostolates often fail to
achieve because of their limited audience. The assembly would
supply the vital need for detailed knowledge and personal contact between authority and execution within the Church.

3. SHARING RESOURCES

One expected result of a national synod bringing together clerical and lay delegates from every diocese in the country would
be the initiation of a discussion on how to begin a long overdue
pooling of resources among American dioceses.

The over-concentration of resources in certain areas was
recognized by the council as a problem requiring a proportionate
distribution of personnel and resources.

4. In November of 1868 Father Isaac Hecker called for a national assembly of the American Church involving both laity and clergy in the discussion of social and economic problems. See "Shall We Have a Catholic
Congress?" *Catholic World*, November, 1868. Two such congresses were
held in Baltimore (1889) and Chicago (1893). Both congresses were
regarded as successes in their effort to delineate lay responsibility in the
area of social action. It is unfortunate that the practice of a national con-
vocation of clergy and laity jointly considering the major problems of the
Church was not continued. See Aaron Abell, *American Catholicism and
Social Action: A Search for Social Justice, 1865-1950* (New York, 1960),
pp. 104 ff.

For a diocese to fulfill its purpose the nature of the Church must be clearly evident to the people of God who constitute that diocese. To this end also bishops must be able to carry out their pastoral duties effectively among their people. Finally, the welfare of the people of God must be served as perfectly as possible.

All this demands, then, a proper determination of the boundaries of dioceses and a distribution of clergy and resources that is reasonable and in keeping with the needs of the apostolate (DCP 22).

A map indicating the current geographical distribution of financial, institutional and personnel resources among the various dioceses in the United States would reveal many curious imbalances. Certain dioceses are over-endowed with a surplus of income and personnel, while others are desperately short of basic requirements for the apostolate. A vocation-rich diocese may assign priests to teach mathematics in its high schools, while a neighboring diocese may not have sufficient priests to staff its parishes adequately.

To some extent this situation is due to the Council of Trent's insistence on the practice of incardination (that is, assigning personnel to a life-long, definite commitment within a particular diocese). This policy, which was adopted as a reaction to abuses resulting from a wandering clergy prior to the Reformation, has long outlived its usefulness, and in many cases impedes the fulfillment of the obvious needs of the Church. In the distribution of their personnel the religious orders transcend diocesan borders, but among the dioceses themselves there is no tradition of pooling resources for mutual projects. Vatican II clearly indicated the necessity of establishing a more flexible deployment of personnel.

Present norms of incardination and excardination should be so revised that while this ancient institution still remains intact, they will better correspond to today's pastoral needs. When a real apostolic spirit requires it, not only should a better distribution of priests be brought about but there should also be favored such pastoral works as are necessary in any region or nation anywhere on earth (DPL 10).

The current status of the Newman Club apostolate (the program of Christian formation for Catholic students attending secular universities) is one of several unfortunate results of the absence of a pattern of shared responsibility among dioceses. As an apostolate which crosses diocesan lines (a state university may be located in one diocese but will draw students from several dioceses), Newman Clubs are almost in a no-man's land regarding the assignment of ecclesiastical personnel. The result is that many of today's Newman Clubs are shoestring operations hopelessly understaffed and underfinanced[5]; a diocesan high school may have twenty or thirty priests assigned to several hundred students while a nearby university with several thousand Catholic students has the service of possibly one or two priests. The ratio of religious to students on Catholic college campuses is one to thirty-five; on secular campuses it is one to thirty-one hundred. And there are over a thousand United States colleges and universities without any Newman program.[6]

The absence of a sense of over-all responsibility also means that individual efforts are permitted to dissipate energy into

5. On the basis of a financial questionnaire in which 85 Newman chaplains participated, Father Thomas Phelan concluded that "the Newman apostolate is generally on a hand-to-mouth, often extremely precarious, financial operation on most campuses. Other agencies, especially Catholic schools, get prime financial status in diocesan programs, the Newman apostolate having a status of economic inferiority"—*The Catholic Herald Citizen*, August 14, 1965.

6. "It is almost impossible to account for the incredibly meager aid which the American Church is giving her half-million sons and daughters on secular campuses. It is almost as if they simply weren't there. The Catholic Almanac for 1962, for example, devotes a number of pages to a complete statistical study, state by state, of the entire Catholic school system. It has not a single word about the half-million Catholics at secular colleges, not to mention the more than 3.3 million (1959) in public elementary or high schools"—Michael Novak, *A New Generation* (New York: Herder and Herder, 1964), pp. 184-185.

relatively unprofitable endeavors. The existence of almost 100 Catholic colleges with less than 55 students and over 200 seminaries with less than 50 candidates indicates that vital personnel are being confined to positions of minimal effectiveness. And programs requiring special knowledge and organizational competency (as the CCD program of religious formation for students outside the Catholic school system) show a considerable variation in quality from diocese to diocese because of the restriction of the most talented personnel to one particular area while a neighboring area must rely on considerably less competent direction.

Thus it would seem that a prime responsibility of a national assembly of the American Church would be a comprehensive review of the extent of ecclesiastical resources, and a comparison of the effectiveness of their current deployment. This review of available resources would naturally lead to a collective decision regarding their future deployment.

> Episcopal conferences should take common counsel to deal with weightier questions and urgent problems, without, however, neglecting local differences. Lest the already insufficient supply of men and means be further dissipated, or lest projects be multiplied without necessity, it is recommended that they [episcopal conferences] pool their resources to found projects which will serve the good of all (DMA 31).

The *Decree on the Missionary Activity of the Church* has a section referring to the obligation which bishops have to establish some sort of norm to determine the specific contribution of each diocese to the general welfare of the Church. The reference is directed specifically to the mission needs of the Church, but it would seem to be equally applicable to the need for an equitable distribution of resources within a nation.

> In their own conferences, the bishops should deliberate about dedicating to the evangelization of the nations some

priests from among the diocesan clergy; they should decide
what definite offering each diocese should be obliged to set
aside annually for the work of the missions, in proportion
to its own budget (DMA 38).

Decisions regarding a more efficient utilization of nation-
wide resources will be effective only if they are *collective* decisions in which all the potential contributors participate, that is,
the smaller dioceses as well as the larger archdioceses, the
smaller religious orders as well as the largest. A reversal of the
current tendency to exclude subordinate groups from the high-
level machinery of ecclesiastical decision-making is as important on the national level as it is on the local level if maximum
response is to be expected throughout the entire Church. Dioceses with endowments above a national norm agreed upon by
all could be expected to contribute of their largess to a common
clearing house for reassignment based on actual need as determined by a commission of evaluation. In a similar manner the
national assembly could provide the framework within which all
the major religious orders of men and women would analyze and
coordinate their national efforts, which have a recognized
tendency to overlap.

> This Synod favors conferences or councils of major supe-
> riors, established by the Holy See. These can contribute
> very much to achieve the purpose of each institute; to
> encourage more effective cooperation for the welfare of the
> Church; to ensure a more just distribution of ministers of
> the Gospel in a given area; and finally to conduct affairs of
> interest to all Religious. Suitable coordination and coopera-
> tion with episcopal conferences should be established with
> regard to the exercise of the apostolate (DOA 23).

Theoretically it would be possible for the respective superiors of these orders to make decisions leading to a coordination
of efforts without consulting a national assembly. But such decisions would be made without the benefit of a total view ascer-

tainable from the wide experience of delegates from every diocese.[7] On the basis of joint decisions regarding the comprehensive needs of the American Church, those religious orders with a heavy concentration of effort in a low-yield endeavor could be expected to initiate an orderly transfer of resources to a higher priority assignment. The various orders of men and women could more effectively direct their particular apostolates through accepting commitments received through national decisions, rather than the present practice of making fragmentized contracts with many individual dioceses.

A national assembly held every two years would also offer to religious orders of men and women the opportunity to evaluate their deployment of resources continuously, in response to the changing needs of the Church. Every community would be able to offer its particular insight into future programs requiring a sharing of ideas and efforts.

> The institutes engaged in missionary activity in the same territory should find ways and means of coordinating their work. Therefore, it will be very useful to have conferences of Religious men and unions of Religious women, in which all institutes of the same country or region should take part. These conferences should ask what things can be done by combined efforts, and they should be in close touch with the episcopal conferences (DMA 33).

The various secular institutes, which through independent initiative have significantly contributed to the quality of Catholic life in the United States, would also have the benefit of a constant re-examination of their particular apostolate in the light of the immediate needs of the Church as determined through the national assembly. The assembly in turn would provide a forum by which these under-publicized institutes could bring their

7. For an examination of various techniques of conducting pastoral projects on a national level, see Francois Houtart and Walter Goddyn, O.F.M., "Problems of Pastoral Organization," in *The Pastoral Mission of the Church,* Concilium, Vol. 3 (Glen Rock, N. J.: The Paulist Press, 1965).

work to the attention and support of the entire membership of the Church.

> Secular Institutes although not Religious institutes involve a true and full profession of the evangelical counsels in the world. This profession is recognized by the Church and consecrates to God men and women, lay and clerical, who live in the world. Hence they should make a total dedication of themselves to God in perfect charity their chief aim, and the institutes themselves should preserve their own proper, i.e., secular character, so that they may be able to carry out effectively everywhere in and, as it were, from the world the apostolate for which they were founded (DOA 11).

It would seem reasonable to expect that a collective analysis of the resources and the problems of the American Church by all involved would lead to concerted action, bringing together apostolic energy from many sources.[8] The overdue pooling of resources of various organizations and communities could send teams of priests, sisters and laity to secular campuses to replace the fragmentary pattern of previous efforts. Collective decisions could lead to a more effective, long range development of the Newman apostolate by forming teams of clergy and laity actually engaged as teachers in various departments of each university.[9] As a dynamic part of the university life and the secular

8. "In the United States the Newman Clubs are very active at many secular universities, and they have gained in importance in the past few years; but they are all directed by priests. Why not think of work in this line for Sisters? . . . It would seem that the very first requirement for a Sister in this field should be a university degree, and if at all possible one from a secular university. This is to assure her position as a woman, rather than as a religious. Her social status must be built up on the fact that she is one of the group, an equal, one who has lived through the experience of an education in the university—not as a matter of pride, but as a basis for mutual respect and understanding"—Francois Houtart, *The Challenge to Change* (New York: Sheed and Ward, 1964), p. 183.

9. For a consideration of alternate proposals regarding the apostolate to the secular campus, see John J. Kirvan, C.S.P., "The Newman Apostolate Is Not Enough," *The Catholic World*, August, 1965. Father Kirvan, a

milieu, they would be far superior to imported personnel occupying a peripheral position on the campus.

> The pastors of the Church are to expend their energies not only on the spiritual life of students who attend Catholic universities, but, solicitous for the spiritual formation of all their children, they must see to it, after consultations between bishops, that even at universities that are not Catholic there should be associations and university centers under Catholic auspices in which priests, religious and laity, carefully selected and prepared, should give abiding spiritual and intellectual assistance to the youth of the university (DCE 10).

The team concept of priests, sisters and laity from various organizations and communities working in voluntary association on specialized programs would be similarly useful for other projects requiring a combined effort among dioceses. The problems of the American Church are immense, but so are its resources, if they can be properly channeled into the most productive outlets. The analysis and fully productive employment of existing resources could conceivably constitute a greater overall accomplishment than the relatively unproductive use of additional resources of personnel and finances.

As a result of decisions made by the national synod, there could be initiated policies and practices designed to assist in the pooling of resources. Denial of academic recognition could be used to prevent further duplication of existing educational facilities, as determined by a national commission. A common fund, possibly obtained by an annual Sunday collection throughout the nation, could be established to provide matching funds to small institutions wishing to combine facilities into larger, more pro-

---

Newman chaplain at Wayne State University in Detroit, considers the Newman movement as only one method of accepting the Church's responsibility on the American campus.

ductive institutions: for example, every dollar raised by four or five religious orders intending to establish a central training institute to replace their isolated efforts would be matched by an equivalent amount from the common fund.

> It is recommended that they [episcopal conferences] pool their resources to found projects which will serve the good of all: as for instance, seminaries; technical schools and schools of higher learning; pastoral, catechetical, and liturgical centers; as well as the means of social communication (DMA 31).

The discussions and consideration of future projects by the delegates of an assembly could be expected to lead to the establishment of programs of research, a need recognized by the council as vital if the Church is to be effective within society.[10] A collective approach to research would be far more likely to succeed in fulfilling the council's expectations than individual efforts of various dioceses.

> The forms of the apostolate should be properly adapted to the needs of the present day with regard not only for man's spiritual and moral circumstances but also for his social, demographic, and economic conditions. Religious and social research, through offices of pastoral sociology, contributes much to the efficacious and fruitful attainment of that goal, and it is highly recommended (DCP 17).

10. A Center for Applied Research in the Apostolate (CARA) was incorporated in August of 1964 by a joint organization including representatives from the Conferences of Major Superiors, the National Council of Catholic Men, the National Council of Catholic Women, the Serra International and other organizations. Under the direction of Louis J. Luzbetak, S.V.D., its goal will be "to discover, promote and apply modern techniques and scientific informational resources for practical use in the Church's social and religious mission in the modern world." (See *The Catholic Directory*, Archdiocese of Washington, 1966.) Immediate projects of CARA include 1) a study of the difficulties in the recruitment and perseverance of religious vocations; 2) the impact of religious on slum areas; 3) the Church in the changing city. CARA's overall effort in research has been somewhat handicapped by the absence of a definite source of financial support; each project depends on whatever funds are available from private gifts and foundation grants.

The spirit of cooperation exemplified in a national synod would tend to produce a similar mentality on a regional basis. Statewide or regional conferences could be established to provide a more efficient administration of resources within a particular area. For example, in place of the pointless duplication of educational offices in neighboring dioceses there could be a single structure pooling and coordinating the resources of the area. This statewide or regional machinery would be so structured as to enable all participants and institutions to determine collectively the policy and the direction of their combined efforts. Regional rather than individual diocesan offices would centralize the most talented personnel where they could be of the greatest service and would also enable the combined resources to be allotted on the basis of the greatest need.

The national synod would not preempt the tradition of national conventions of particular apostolates or organizations. The latter would continue to convene, but they would have the benefit of knowing that their discussions and reports, which were formerly confined to a somewhat limited audience, could now be representatively presented at a national assembly of delegates from every diocese in the United States.

By providing an open forum for the presentation of initiative and new projects within the Church, a national assembly could encourage the type of independent response desired by Vatican II.

> For in the Church there are many apostolic undertakings which are established by the free choice of the laity and regulated by their prudent judgment. The mission of the Church can be better accomplished in certain circumstances by undertakings of this kind, and therefore they are frequently praised or recommended by the hierarchy (DOL 24).

One example of a particularly beneficial form of apostolic undertaking made by free choice within the Church would be the formation of a national catechetical conference. The problem of finding adequate answers to the catechetical problems now facing the Church—for example, the Christian formation of students outside the Catholic school system, the better adaptation of the message to the mentality of its recipients, among others—will require bold experimentation and charismatic endowments of insight and administrative initiative which the official Church, with its present structure, is incapable of developing.

Thus it would be to the interest of the entire Church if the national synod were to encourage recognized catechetical authorities to form an independent catechetical conference which could analyze objectively the nation's program of religious formation inside and outside the school system, and which would place its collective reputation behind recommendations and techniques leading to improvement.[11] Eventually, the official Church could incorporate the insights and the wisdom of the catechetical conferences in a manner similar to its recent incorporation of the experience and wisdom of the independent national Liturgical Conference.[12] The council spoke of possible benefits of this type of conference.

> This sacred synod also prescribes that general directories be prepared treating of the care of souls for the use of both bishops and pastors. Thus they will be provided with certain methods which will help them to discharge their own pastoral office with greater ease and effectiveness.
>
> There should be prepared also a particular directory concerning the pastoral care of special groups of the faithful as

11. *The Church's Educational Ministry: A Curriculum Plan* (Bethany Press, 848 pp.) is the result of five years of cooperative catechetical study by 16 Protestant denominations of the latest trends in educational philosophy and theological thought. Prepared by 150 specialists in religious education, the document deals with the objectives of religious education and provides a guide for relating the central religious themes to various age levels.

12. For indications of the pioneering efforts of the Liturgical Conference, see the proceedings of the annual liturgical weeks published by The Liturgical Conference, Washington, D. C.

the different circumstances of individual nations or regions require. Another directory should be composed concerning the catechetical instruction of the Christian people; this directory will consider the fundamental principles of such instruction, its disposition and the composition of books on the subject (DCP 44).

4. EQUALITY OF REPRESENTATION

A number of technical changes would have to be made to establish equality of representation among the various dioceses within the national synod. This could reasonably be expected to result from a division of today's largest dioceses. The *Decree on the Pastoral Offices of Bishops* indicates what a diocese should be.

> The extent of the diocese and the number of its inhabitants should generally be such that, on the one hand, the bishop himself—even though assisted by others—can officiate at pontifical functions, make pastoral visitations, faithfully direct and coordinate all the works of the apostolate in the diocese and know well especially his priests, and also the religious and lay people who are engaged in diocesan projects (DCP 23 [2]).

It is obvious that this standard does not fit a number of the largest American dioceses. Even new administrative structures permitting communication and participation will not be remedial in certain areas. Only the establishment of smaller diocesan units will permit the respective bishop to be discernible to the faithful as the father and guide which the council intends.

> Concerning diocesan boundaries, therefore, this sacred synod decrees that, to the extent required by the good of souls, a fitting revision of diocesan boundaries be undertaken prudently and as soon as possible. This can be done by dividing, dismembering or uniting them, or by changing their boundaries, or by determining a better place for the episcopal see or, finally, especially in the case of dioceses having larger cities, by providing them with a new internal organization (DCP 22).

In the United States this would conceivably involve the creation of fifty or sixty new dioceses over which the present auxiliary bishops could be expected to preside.[13] In expanding urban areas it would seem advisable to replace the traditional arrangement (one archbishop with two or three auxiliary bishops under his direction) with a "college" of bishops, each bishop having a definite territory but acting in concert under the collegiate presidency of the archbishop of the area. Thus the episcopal situation in the large urban areas of the future would be a smaller projection of the national situation where a more democratic sharing of authority among bishops can be expected to exist.

Of course it would be a unique experience to discuss the problems of the American Church in an open national assembly, especially when there is a long tradition in the United States of making high-level ecclesiastical decisions without a pattern of consultation. Many who are accustomed to the pre-Vatican II habit of arriving at serene decisions in closed sessions will undoubtedly experience the same anxiety felt by a number of prelates over the pattern of open discussion adopted by Vatican II.

But in view of the obvious success of an open presentation of opposing views within the universal assembly of Vatican II, is it legitimately possible to question the value of the same method within a national assembly? Vatican II has clearly stated that religious are to undertake their works in the apostolate only through mutual collaboration with the bishops.

13. For an analysis of the structural problems of the Church in England, see A. E. C. W. Spencer, "The Structure and Organization of the Catholic Church in England," in *Uses of Sociology*, edited by J. D. Halloran and Joan Brothers (London: Sheed and Ward, 1966). Spencer foresees a steady decrease in the effectiveness of Church leadership as long as it insists on preserving the present episcopal-clerical monopoly of leadership roles and denies Church members any participation in the influence- and decision-making processes.

For those works of the apostolate which religious are to undertake, bishops or episcopal conferences, religious superiors or conferences of major religious superiors should take action only after mutual consultations.

In order to foster harmonious and fruitful mutual relations between bishops and religious, at stated times and as often as it is deemed opportune, bishops and religious superiors should meet to discuss those affairs which pertain to the apostolate in their territory (DCP 35 [5-6]).

It would seem to be a matter of simple justice that the same type of consultation occur in regard to the particular apostolate of the laity. The Holy Spirit through the Vatican Council has given the highest endorsement to synods and councils.

This sacred Ecumenical Synod earnestly desires that the venerable institution of synods and councils flourish with fresh vigor. In such a way faith will be deepened and discipline preserved more fittingly and efficaciously in the various Churches, as the needs of the times require (DCP 36).

Given the extent of lay commitment in the American Church, would it be reasonable to expect that a synod or council would be effective in the United States without a representative sampling of the entire faithful?[14]

It is difficult to see how the full weight of the American Church's wisdom and energy can be brought to bear on the complex situation of the Christian today unless this situation is presented directly to the Church by those who daily live in it. The exchange of opinion between hierarchy and faithful which occurs through informal contacts and discussion is valuable to the extent that the number of faithful involved is sufficiently large to convey the different views of the people of God, a difficult achievement without some type of machinery facilitating the authentic delivery of varying opinions.

The leading Catholic periodicals and a revitalized diocesan

14. For a review of the role of the laity in conciliar history, see Hans Küng, *Structures of the Church*, pp. 74 ff.

press (possibly one newspaper jointly produced by three or four dioceses, rather than the talent-dissipating goal of a paper in every diocese) can provide an open forum for mutually profitable encounters between the charismatic and the organizational elements of the Church.[15] But there remains a basic need for a structured, authentically representative exchange of views and opinions among those making decisions and those informed Christians who have alternate possibilities to be considered. This type of encounter cannot be a constant factor in the life of the Church. Its availability, however, at the appropriate times and in an effective format remains as the final test of how open the Church is to the Spirit revealed through the voices of the faithful.[16]

A national synod would offer one possibility of representatively involving the laity in the overall direction of apostolic efforts on a nation-wide basis. But it would also be necessary to devise structures utilizing the full potential of lay involvement in the specific implementation of the synod's directives. The *Decree Concerning the Pastoral Office of Bishops in the Church* refers to the machinery which the bishops and the faithful of a nation may use to guide apostolic effort.

> Each episcopal conference is to draft its own statutes for recognition by the Apostolic See. In these statutes, among other things, offices should be established which will aid in achieving its purpose more efficaciously, for example, a permanent board of bishops, episcopal commissions and a general secretariat (DCP 38 [3]).

15. See Msgr. S. J. Adamo, "Dilemma in the Catholic Press," *America*, August 14, 1965.

16. "The problems of public policy, race, organization, neighborhoods, ecumenical dialogue, poverty, mobility, the family, public safety, to mention but a few, require constant thought and attention as to just how the Christian message, the fire of Christian charity, shall effectively be brought to bear. In many of these instances, the laity and only the laity have the beginning of answers"—"Interim Report on the Greater Participation and Involvement of the Laity in the Life and Work of the Church."

This passage is frequently interpreted as an indirect compliment to the American Church, whose bishops prior to Vatican II had evolved a pattern of cooperation which included the elements now recognized as beneficial: an administrative board, various episcopal commissions and a general secretariat. In 1919 the American bishops formed a nation-wide voluntary association of bishops which they called the National Catholic Welfare Conference or NCWC. It was a service organization intended to coordinate various aspects of Catholic activities in the United States voluntarily. It was nominally under the direction of the entire American episcopate, but in practice it was directed by the small number of senior prelates who held positions on its administrative board.

In the intervening years the NCWC has grown to the extent that it now has over 200 clerical and lay employees working in a ten-story building in Washington, D. C. Through its various departments and bureaus, the NCWC attempts to implement the bishops' wishes and to coordinate nation-wide activities in the field of ecumenism, the liturgy, lay and youth organizations, congressional lobbying, and social action, to name only a few. Its world-wide relief service has had a distinguished record in channeling clothing, food and medicine to the needy throughout the world.

On the surface, the NCWC would appear to be an ideal tool to serve as the coordinating agency for the collective efforts of the American Church. It has both a tradition and a staff of proven efficiency. Its social action and its lay organization departments have functioned well as a clearing house and a coordinator of programs throughout the nation. And it continues to respond with flexibility to the requests of the bishops.

But what was an effective instrument prior to Vatican II may require restructuring to meet the collegiate pattern of activity desired by the council. The NCWC secretariat, with its various departments, was originally a private creation of the bishops. Although the organization is reasonably efficient in executing the directions given to it by the bishops, it has no machinery for soliciting and coordinating the suggestions of the lower clergy and laity—a fact appreciated by the many United States bishops desirous of reforming this structure. Several of its departments utilize experts efficiently, but other departments lack both the personnel and the finances to do an effective job. As the bishops' service organization in the United States, the secretariat follows the mandate directions supplied by the relatively small number of bishops occupying positions on the administrative board. The absence of a tradition of selecting representatively the episcopal members of the all-important and all-controlling administrative board considerably narrows the organization's ability to bring the wisdom and energy of all bishops to bear on Church problems in the United States.

Under the influence of the renewal emenating from Vatican II, the NCWC may evolve into a pattern of activity immensely beneficial to the American Church. But the purely appointive nature of its key administrative positions and its confinement of responsibility to a select group constitute serious hazards in achieving shared responsibility throughout the American Church. Basically, the NCWC faces the same problems with which chanceries and curias must always contend: appointed officials whose work is not subject to total review and whose primary responsibility is to their respective appointer.

The bishops of Vatican II preferred to elect candidates to key commission positions rather than silently accept untested nominees. It would seem reasonable to presume that the entire American episcopate would prefer to participate actively in the selection of individuals occupying positions within the American Church somewhat similar to the positions occupied by commission members at Vatican II. Probably, too, most bishops would prefer to have their own judgment in this regard aided by the discerning wisdom of competent laity.

Perhaps this could best be achieved by having the key NCWC officials selected every two years by the national synod. The heads of departments and bureaus of the revised general secretariat would report directly to the assembly on the goals and accomplishments of their organizations during the preceding two years. Individuals of recognized competence could be selected to head special commissions entrusted with executing the will of the general assembly during the coming two years, while the sunlight of an open review of the successes and failures of the Church's attempt at implementing its wisdom would bring new energy to its work. Thus the NCWC would become to the national synod what the Roman curia should be to the universal synod: a general secretariat responsible for executing the desires of the assembly, and subject to its review regarding both its methods and its personnel. To allow either secretariat to continue to operate with only a limited responsibility to certain key officials is to seriously jeopardize what should be the superior status of the synods, which are intended to be the authentic channels of the Church's wisdom.

It will be helpful to recall that Vatican II ignited large quantities of Christian enthusiasm and energy because it offered the ideal opportunity to publicize the problems and the goals of the Church through an extensive use of the communications media. The council specifically requested the same type of publicity for the problems and concerns of the Church within each nation.

> Since an effective apostolate on a national scale calls for unity of planning and resources, this sacred Synod decrees and orders that national offices for affairs of the press, films, radio and television be established everywhere and given every aid (DMS 21).

In the *Decree Concerning the Pastoral Office of Bishops,* the fathers also recognized the value of press and TV coverage of their meetings and statements.

They should also strive to make use of the various media at hand nowadays for proclaiming Christian doctrine, . . . conferences, and meetings of every kind, and finally its dissemination through public statements at times of outstanding events as well as by the press and various other media of communication, which by all means ought to be used in proclaiming the Gospel of Christ (DCP 13).

But it should be obvious that there is an obligation incumbent on the Church itself to create the situation to which the communications media can turn for a concentrated presentation of the full life of the Church. A national synod could reasonably be expected to draw sufficient coverage in all the news media to stimulate the public interest and concern which Vatican II achieved on an international level, and which is equally vital on a national level if renewal is to succeed.

Once again it may be said that the hierarchy's willingness to adopt new structures permitting the faithful to participate effectively in the national life of the Church will be the great revealer of the extent of our trust in the Spirit's way of operating through the faithful. In Vatican II the Holy Spirit has indicated its desire for the maximum utilization of the charismatic endowment of the entire people of God. Can we really expect the faithful to exercise initiative, and to bring all their divine energy to bear on the national problems of the Church, without some form of open discussion prior to decisions?

It was in America that men for the first time made and mastered on a nation-wide basis the need to maintain within the same social organism the principles of centralism and federalism, unity and pluralism, acceptance and criticism, consensus and dissent. The future of the American Church may well be determined by its collective ability to utilize this natural endowment as a basis for its incarnation.[17] One of Pope John's gifts to man-

17. The closing lines of "Father Hecker's Farewell Sermon," preached at St. Paul the Apostle Church, New York City, Sunday, October 17, 1869, previous to his departure for the First Vatican Council:

kind was his recognition that Christianity can best approach the problems of the world after Christians have had the opportunity to present their experience and their insights to one another in an open council. It would seem reasonable to presume that the wisdom, energy and enthusiasm for renewal resulting from the frank study of problems within the open assembly of Vatican II would be paralleled by similar results from an open assembly in our own nation.

I desire you to look forward, as I do, to a new and glorious era in the Church's history, an era of faith and holiness, in which I trust our own country is destined to become the theater of a brilliant development of the Catholic Religion. I earnestly recommend to your prayers the success of the great work which is before the council, and my own prosperous return to you after its close (*The Catholic World*, Vol. 10, December, 1869, p. 293).

Chapter Five

THE INTERNATIONAL SCENE:
A MEDITERRANEAN CHURCH
OR A CHURCH OF ALL NATIONS?

Is the United Nations more international than the Roman Catholic Church? In certain respects it would seem that in the years prior to Vatican II the world organization located in New York was far more international in its composition and its administration than the world society centered in Rome.

The Church had always recognized its international nature; one, holy, *catholic* and apostolic has been for several centuries the traditional expression of its universal tendency. But in the pre-Vatican II era there were many observers who did not clearly perceive this internationalism. Prior to the opening of the council, secular journals frequently expressed the hope that it would succeed in making the Church less Roman and more Catholic, and that its world direction would cease to be an Italian domestic affair.[1]

Of course the council itself gave impressive proof of the international element of the Church. Bishops from almost every nation in the world adopted a pattern of equal and open discussion of their mutual problems. In their analysis of the overall

1. "At first sight the meaning 'international' and the meaning 'catholic' are the same. On closer inspection the reality appears very different. The lack of an international sense among Catholics is very obvious"—Francois Houtart, "The Church and International Responsibility," *Act*, September, 1965.

situation, the vast majority of the participants repeatedly urged an internationalization of the machinery of ecclesiastical management. And the council indirectly advanced the process of internationalizing the Church by providing talented prelates from many nations with the opportunity to display a knowledge of the modern world, and the Church's current situation in it, that was considerably more comprehensive than that of many domestic occupants within its power structure.

The problem now facing the Church is how to maintain a similar international discussion, with its obvious benefits, at a time when its internationally-minded prelates are not united in assembly. Of almost equal importance is the related problem: How is the Church to continue the internationalization of its central management, which was begun under the pressure of the full assembly of bishops and which must now be advanced when the internationally-minded have departed from Rome?

Both problems are formidable. There is no precedent to serve as a guideline in developing horizontal patterns of communication and exchange of views among the bishops throughout the world other than the traditional, vertical link directly connecting each bishop with the central administrative offices or curia in Rome. Although every council since Basil and Constance (over 500 years ago) has recommended that this curia (the inner corps of papal advisors directing various administrative departments in Rome) should be international in its personnel and its structure, no council has ever succeeded in this goal.[2] If in the immediate post-Vatican II years there is no successful effort to establish lines of representative contact among the bishops of the world, it is possible that the weight of tradition could reproduce a continuation of the pre-conciliar pattern of Mediterranean management.

2. For a general history of the councils, see Philip Hughes, *The Church in Crisis: A History of the General Councils, 325-1870* (Garden City: Hanover House, 1961).

Effective solutions to these problems cannot be delayed. The council has produced a series of reforming documents in liturgy, ecumenism, the missionary apostolate, to name only a few, but these documents could conceivably become mere position papers, frequently ignored in the daily practice of the Church, if they are to be officially interpreted by a cast of advisers with a mental attitude different from that of the authors of the documents. The sobering experience of council sessions in which a very small number of curia officials repeatedly frustrated the obvious desires of the vast majority of bishops should serve as a warning. An open door, international Church cannot be considered as an automatic achievement of the conciliar documents. Internationalization of the Church will be achieved only if an open discussion of its life can be maintained on an international basis, and if internationally responsive individuals occupy the key advisory and administerial positions within it.

Reference has been made earlier to the council's transfer of certain powers from curia offices to the various episcopal conferences throughout the world—for example, the power to make liturgical decisions affecting a particular nation, and the control of seminary education. This effort at reversing the centralizing trend dominant within the Church in the centuries after Trent constitutes a most significant advance in that it gives new power to bishops previously outside the central power structure. It also offers the prospect of having the various episcopal conferences serve as a counter-balance to the non-international views of those geographically closer to the papal office.

In certain respects, the enlargement of the College of Cardinals contributed to the internationalizing process.[3] The conferral of the cardinalate honor upon a large number of prelates outside the Vatican had the obvious effect of adding an officially

3. For a commentary on the mixed reactions to the appointment of new cardinals in the Spring of 1965 and its effect on ecumenical relations with Orthodox Catholics, see Thomas E. Bird, "Red Hats As Red Flags," *Commonweal*, March 26, 1965.

approved status to a significant number of international leaders beyond the inner corps of traditional advisers living in Rome. It also had the generally overlooked but important effect of reducing the prestige of ecclesiastical dignitaries within the Church through the multiple diffusion of honors previously confined to a select few. As an honorary office limited to administerial bishops in Rome and a relatively small number of other prelates throughout the world, the cardinalate could have presented several problems in the post-conciliar era. Any continuation of the pre-conciliar practice of having the cardinal (or senior cardinal) of a nation assume the key position of chairman in his episcopal conference would have given a few officials within the Vatican a secondary but effective lever of control over national hierarchies when the latter inevitably expanded in size beyond the capacity of a pope to make a completely independent selection of a nation's cardinal.

But in another sense, it is difficult to visualize the benefits gained from the continuation of a position which has the unfortunate tendency to establish an artificial distinction among members of the hierarchy. The practice of bestowing ceremonial honors of dress and position on certain bishops purely on the basis of personal appointment was unknown throughout the greater part of Christian history. There is good reason to believe that a practice adopted during the Renaissance should be discontinued in a modern era which does not place great value on the court display and the symbolic exuberance of an earlier age. The desired internationalization of the Church would undoubtedly be better served if the bestowal of honorary distinctions among bishops by a central authority were replaced by a system conferring authentic leadership positions on certain bishops within a region on the basis of a collective evaluation by their associates.[4]

4. For a discussion on the effects of a continued use of the appointive system in selecting cardinals and other Church leaders, see Joseph O'Donoghue, "Elections in the Church," *Commonweal*, May 21, 1965.

1. THE CONTINUING COUNCIL

In this regard it is important to note that one of the most encouraging elements in the newly established universal synod of bishops is the fact that an elective process will be used to determine membership.[5] During the council there had been a steadily growing expectation that those bishops who had been selected by their fellow bishops to represent their collective position on various issues would continue to exercise their beneficial influence within the Church through some form of "senate" after the council had concluded. Various bishops had repeatedly asked for a senate in their council speeches, and on several occasions Pope Paul had promised to establish it.

History may record that the most significant aspect of the episcopal synod or senate of bishops, as finally announced by the pope, was the *elective* element implicit in its structure. The international members of the synod are to be determined by the various episcopal conferences themselves, the actual number of representatives from each conference being determined by its size (that is, a 25-member conference has one representative in the synod, a 50-member conference has two, a 100-member conference has three, a 200-member conference has four). The value of the elective process in determining the membership of the episcopal senate can hardly be overestimated. An appointive procedure of selecting members could have resulted in an assembly which was international to the extent that its peninsular appointers wished to be international. The use of the elective process by all the episcopal conferences of the world should mean that their representatives will again bring to Rome

5. "The Synod of Bishops, whereby the bishops chosen from various parts of the world lend their valuable assistance to the Supreme Pastor of the Church, is so constituted as to be: a) a central ecclesiastical institution; b) representing the complete Catholic episcopate; c) by its nature perpetual; d) and as for its structure, performing its duties for a time and when called upon." See *Apostolica Sollicitudo,* the motu proprio of Pope Paul VI establishing a synod of bishops.

the type of internationalism which they themselves brought to the Vatican Council.

Of almost equal importance is the factor of independent judgment which elected representatives can be expected to exhibit within the episcopal synod. In the past, the talented and ambitious bishops within a nation who wished a greater share of responsibility within the universal Church could be expected to reflect the Roman viewpoint and to adopt the curia policy. In the future, these same bishops will be inclined to serve as spokesmen for the collegiate wisdom of the bishops of their own nation. The use of the elective process in determining the bishops who will represent a conference will make potential synod candidates among the bishops most responsive to each bishop within the conference, who will now be regarded as an elector to be listened to rather than a subordinate associate of the senior bishop. The internationalization of the Church will be considerably advanced when each episcopal conference sends to its universal synod elected representatives bearing the wisdom achieved by regional deliberations, rather than the previously proclaimed wisdom of the central authority.

As originally announced, the function of the senate will be to inform and to advise the pope, and to exercise the measure of deliberative power assigned to it by the pontiff.[6] How international the Church becomes may well depend on whether this synod can evolve into a general assembly representative of the entire Church, with a rotating membership and functioning as a permanent council with the pope as final ratifier of its discussions. The achievement of this type of a permanent council could be a significant factor in recovering that sense of common solicitude for all the Churches and for all mankind which was a vital

---

6. "II. By its very nature it is the task of the Synod of Bishops to inform and give advice. It may also have deliberative power, when such power is conferred on it by the sovereign Pontiff, who will in such cases confirm the decisions of the synod"—*ibid.*

element in the early Church. This universal concern of the early Christians was the result of their general awareness of the collegiate nature of the Church as revealed in the Christian proclamation and as concretized in the practice of frequent synods and councils, which drew personnel from many areas for the purposes of consultation and mutual deliberation.

> From the very first centuries of the Church bishops, as rulers of individual Churches, were deeply moved by the communion of fraternal charity and zeal for the universal mission entrusted to the Apostles. And so they pooled their abilities and their wills for the common good and for the welfare of the individual Churches. Thus came into being synods, provincial councils and plenary councils in which bishops established for various Churches the way to be followed in teaching the truths of faith and ordering ecclesiastical discipline (DCP 36).

The involvement of men of many nationalities and mentalities in the decision-making apparatus gave the early Church an international attitude more in keeping with its universal mission than the somewhat peninsular attitude of recent centuries, resulting from the dominance of one nation and one mentality in the same decision-making apparatus. It would appear to be obvious that if the Church is to be effectively international in the postconciliar era it will be necessary to have an international assembly as the basis of its pronouncements and decisions.[7]

The practice of making decisions only after some form of international consultation may be somewhat difficult to adopt.

---

7. "In 1888, Father Isaac Hecker of the Paulist Fathers urged that the College of Cardinals become 'the religious senate of the world.' He welcomed the increase of democratic institutions which he felt: '. . . . would result in the College of Cardinals being made a representative body of all mankind. It would be the religious senate of the world. Its decisions would be the decisions of the religious sense of humanity, and whoever would resist them would be ostracized and suffer popular abscission from the Church whether he were formally excommunicated or not"—*The Catholic World,* Vol. 48, No. 283, pp. 10-11.

The imperial and feudal habits of control acquired through the centuries have so deeply affected our way of regarding the Church that it will require the combined efforts of the most creative planners and the most skilled organizers to adapt it to a non-imperial and non-feudal pattern of decision-making. The adaptation is long overdue, and there is a relatively small amount of time in which it can be achieved. The fact that the present council could obtain a fair degree of success under an organizational structure which almost ignored the representative and parliamentary knowledge obtained in modern times should not hide the realization that, within a few years, another council similar to Vatican II (or any one of the previous ecumenical councils) will be a physical impossibility. Between Vatican I and Vatican II the hierarchy expanded from approximately 600 members to almost 3,000; the consequences of a similar increase do not need to be analyzed.

The obvious choice which must now be made is to determine whether the Church and its response to the world will be directed by an oligarchic few or by the representative assembly of the people of God. To ignore the choice or even to delay making an answer could mean that the pattern of overall direction of Church life could evolve into a narrow form of control which no one intended, but which nevertheless could become the dominant pattern of the future. It would be far better to ask ourselves a number of hard and somewhat unfamiliar questions, with a view to determining the future, rather than accept developments which circumstances may force upon us.

For example, would the collegiate nature of the Church be best served by electing the pope for a single, non-repeatable term of ten years? The resignation of earlier popes (for example, Celestine V and Gregory XII) could be regarded as indicating that a lifetime occupancy is not essential to the structuring of the primacy. The strain of the pontifical office, which historically has been a heavy burden, will increase fantastically in the future because of the new obligations of the papal office. Many candidates would probably prefer a ten-year pontificate because of the hope of future release from the burden of office, and there is a possibility that some candidates will be unwilling to accept the office unless it is of limited duration. One result of a limited term for the Supreme Pontiff would be to make infallibility unmistakably manifest as a gift to an *office*, not a person, for the purpose of providing central unity among the people of God.

There are other unfamiliar questions. An annually convened senate would effectively represent the people of God in the decision-making apparatus of the Church. But would the nature of the Church as the family of God in the world be more manifest if all the bishops of the world assembled every ten years on a different continent, in a key city (for example, Bombay, Lima, London, Toronto), possibly on the occasion of a papal election in which all the bishops and a representative sampling of the laity participated? The needed reduction of imperial pageantry,[8] as well as the substitution of more fraternal and understandable symbols of office, could be fringe benefits of an impressive demonstration to the world that Christianity transcends its Mediterranean origin.

It is important to realize that questions regarding the future direction of the Church in the world are questions which the entire people of God should consider. Vatican II is a clear sign that the Church can respond to the communicated wisdom of the faithful. It would be a serious mistake to consider an international direction of its life as a future achievement of the official

8. "The Holy Roman Empire no longer exists, but there still remain in the Church many titles and insignia, many elements of ceremonial and so of her visible aspect, borrowed at some time from the dazzling imperial splendour. Surely it is high time, and surely it would be to everyone's advantage, 'to shake off the dust of the Empire that has gathered since Constantine's day on the throne of St. Peter.' Those words were spoken by John XXIII"—Yves Congar, O.P., *Power and Poverty in the Church* (Baltimore: Helicon, 1964), p. 127.

echelon of the Church. This assumption would be contrary to the actual method of obtaining previous advances in the internationalizing process, and if believed could conceivably inhibit future progress. The synod of bishops resulted from the beneficial pressure exerted by a minority of bishops who originally foresaw its value, and who by deliberately looking for additional support effectively lobbied for its establishment. An international attiude and an international structure can be only indirectly produced by official fiat; the constantly expressed pressure of the common expectation of Christians for an open Church will be the most significant stimulant to further internationalization.

> In exercising this care of souls, pastors and their assistants should so fulfill their duty of teaching, sanctifying and governing that the faithful and the parish communities will truly realize that they are members both of the diocese and of the universal Church (DCP 30).

Representatively structured parishes and dioceses, with interests and projects that transcend geographical confinement, and which thereby constitute a clearly discernible example of universal responsibility among the people of God, are bound to produce a chain-like series of similar expectations throughout the entire Church.[9] Every instance in which individual Christians look beyond their own local concerns to the wider purpose of a Church which transcends national limitations will have a cumulative effect leading to that international incarnation desired by Christ and accepted as a goal by all who bear his name. Each successful effort at creating an open structure anywhere in the Church should be regarded as a beneficial addition to an increasing public expectation, eventually leading to the establishment of open structures at the highest level of ecclesiastical machinery.

Any hesitancy to contribute proposals for the needed enlarge-

9. For a discussion of the lay apostolate around the world, see Meyer, *The Whole World Is My Neighbor*.

ment of ecclesiastical structure and outlook should be countered by the realization that it was a group of thirty clergy and laity in the Archdiocese of St. Louis who, in proposing an open assembly within their archdiocese, exercised an obviously imitable form of initiative. Every instance of this nature, in which a representative direction of large-scale Church effort is suggested and then successfully conducted, serves as a powerful example of the possibility of further representative direction of Church affairs on national and international levels. And it will be profitable to recall that the minority of bishops originally convinced of the value of an international synod probably drew their conviction from contact and dialogue with their own faithful. The overall record of Vatican II should constitute impressive proof that when clearly formulated and specifically expressed, the common expectations of the people of God tend to be incorporated into the life of the Church.[10]

What should our collective expectations be regarding the necessary internationalization of the Church? In the light of Christ's proclamation of a ministry to all nations, and in view of the Spirit-inspired summoning of an ecumenical assembly to facilitate this proclamation, it would seem reasonable to expect Christians to concentrate their efforts on obtaining an international synod of bishops that would serve as a continuing council in the spirit of Vatican II. An episcopal senate annually convened to consider its international problems could be expected to provide general guidelines for Church life throughout the world, and to offer specific Christian responses to the constantly changing world situation.

> Since it [the Synod of Bishops] will be acting in the name of the entire Catholic episcopate, it shall at the same time show that all the bishops in hierarchical communion partake of the solicitude for the universal Church (DCP 5).

10. See Stephen Charles Neill and Hans-Reudi Weber, edd., *The Layman in Christian History* (Philadelphia: The Westminster Press, 1963).

With the pope as their head, the entire body of bishops could (through their elected representatives) continue to proceed as an assembly deliberating together, and deciding doctrinal and pastoral issues in virtue of their collective power. Strictly speaking, the episcopal senate cannot function as a political body or a corporate board, since the holder of the papal office would not be obligated to accept the episcopal consensus in every instance. The Church, the entire episcopate, and the pope himself are truly possessors of supreme power, each in a different way.[11] After many centuries of over-centralized government, it may take several years for all involved to accept fully and sincerely the collegiate way of government, in which all the bishops share joint responsibility for the entire Church. The task of finding a proper balance of power among the various centers of authority will be a delicate process requiring sensitive adjustments and numerous compromises.

The resulting achievement of collegiality, or shared responsibility within the Church, could be the single most far-reaching effect of Vatican II. An authentic execution of collegiality at the top will inspire further efforts at developing a shared sense of responsibility throughout the entire Church. It was mentioned earlier that the primitive Church enjoyed a solicitude for every other Church and for the entire human race, which served as a special stimulus to the Christianization of the world. The reassertion of that attitude in the post-conciliar era may recover for it the dynamic, outward thrust of its early centuries.

2. THE FUTURE OF THE CURIA

Fundamental to the success of the episcopal synod will be a specific delineation of the role which the existing curia will play

11. For an attempt to define the relationship between the episcopacy and the primacy of the Pope, see Wilhelm Bertrams, S.J., *The Papacy, the Episcopacy, and Collegiality* (Westminster, Md.: Newman Press, 1964). Translated by Patrick Brannan, S.J.

in the future life of the Church. In the over-centralized administration of the pre-Vatican II era, the curia was in effect both a
secretariat and a senate. From positions originally intended to
be purely administrative, certain key officials determined Church
policy as effectively as if they were members of the magisterium.

It will require considerable reorganization to make the curia
become what it was intended to be: a service responsible for the
execution of directives given by higher authority in the Church.

> The Fathers of this sacred Council, however, desire that
> these [i.e., curia] departments be reorganized and better
> adapted to the needs of the times, regions, and rites espe-
> cially as regards their number, name, competence and spe-
> cial method of procedure, as well as the coordination of
> work among them (DCP 9).

The fact that a minority of appointed officials in administerial positions could in so many instances block the intentions of
the majority of bishops of Vatican II would seem to suggest the
advisability of having the heads of departments in a reformed
curia elected by the episcopal senate, to which they would be
directly responsible.[12] Major officials within the curia would
hold office on a rotating basis, and would periodically report to
the senate on the execution of their respective functions. The
lesser officials within each department could be determined on
a fixed international proportion similar to the system used to
maintain an international balance among the staff of the United
Nations.

A mathematical proportion in the assignment of minor
offices and staff positions would be essential, to avoid the geographical imbalance which has characterized the bureaucracy
of the Church for the last four hundred years.

> Since these [curia] departments are established for the

---

12. For a report on the "November Crisis" at the close of the third session of the Vatican Council, see Xavier Rynne, *The Third Session* (New
York: Farrar, Straus & Giroux, 1965), pp. 238 ff.

good of the universal Church, it is desirable that their members, officials, and consultors as well as legates of the Roman pontiff be more widely taken from various regions of the Church, insofar as it is possible. In such a way the offices and central organs of the Catholic Church will exhibit a truly universal character (DCP 10).

The offices and services of a secretariat similar to today's curia will always be needed by an international assembly of episcopal delegates, but the de-centralization of Church government can be expected to assign more administerial details to local authorities, and thus help to eliminate the four-century-old practice of having bureau technicians "interpret" the mind of the Holy Father. It might also be helpful to relocate various departments of a reformed curia, in order to facilitate the handling of their particular program—for instance, the Secretariat for Christian Unity could be centered in Geneva to permit maximum cooperation with the World Council of Churches, which has its headquarters there.

The episcopal senate could also be expected to appoint special commissions to direct and to coordinate various efforts of the Church. The *Decree on the Missionary Activity of the Church* refers to the various types of personnel who should be involved in the Congregation of the Propagation of the Faith (the department of the curia responsible for the overall direction of missionary activity). The decree's methodical recognition of the value of widespread consultation, voting privileges for an internationally representative group, and the conferral of authority upon the membership, could be regarded as establishing a model for other congregations and commissions.

In the direction of this office, an active role with a deliberative vote should be had by selected representatives of all those who cooperate in missionary work: that is, the bishops of the whole world in the episcopal conferences should be heard from in this regard, as well as the moderators of pontifical institutes and works, in ways and under conditions to be fixed by the Roman Pontiff. All these, being called together at stated times, will exercise supreme control of all mission work under the authority of the Supreme Pontiff. This office should have available a permanent group of expert consultors, of proven knowledge and experience, whose duty it will be, among other things, to gather pertinent information about local conditions in various regions, and about the thinking of various groups of men, as well as about the means of evangelization to be used. They will then propose scientifically based conclusions for mission work and cooperation (DMA 29).

This proposed composition of the Congregation of the Propagation of the Faith is so novel, in view of the previously restricted membership of the bureau, that it practically constitutes a new commission. Its carefully delineated program of consultation among the proficient, and the use of scientifically obtained information, constitutes a vital precedent to be followed in the creation by the episcopal senate of similar commissions designed to offer specialized assistance in world problems such as world poverty and over-population. The value of a special commission on the problem of world poverty was clearly recognized by the council.

The council, considering the immensity of the hardships which still afflict the greater part of mankind today, regards it as most opportune that an organism of the universal Church be set up in order that both the justice and love of Christ toward the poor might be developed everywhere. The role of such an organism would be to stimulate the Catholic community to promote progress in needy regions and international social justice (PCC 90).

The greater part of the world is still suffering from so much poverty that it is as if Christ Himself were crying out in these poor to beg the charity of the disciples (PCC 88).

A proper sense of collegiality would require that the episcopal senate establish methods of communication by which the various members of the people of God could bring their problems and their services to its attention. Representatives of the religious orders of men and women would be participants in the senate discussions and would inform the assembly of the views and opinions of their respective communities. Clerical and lay consultants would be summoned on matters within their particular competencies, and due recognition would be given to the principle that there should be open hearings permitting maximum communication prior to specific decisions or pronouncements. A conciliar recommendation to the Roman curia would seem to be equally applicable to the episcopal senate.

> It would be most advantageous if these same [curia] departments would listen more attentively to laymen who are outstanding for their virtue, knowledge and experience. In such a way they will have an appropriate share in Church affairs (DCP 10).

The creation of new dioceses wherever necessary, and the combination of others in either de-populated or de-Christianized areas, would be means used to achieve a just balance of representatives from the various episcopal conferences of the world. The senate, however, would not constitute the single framework of communication among the various hierarchies of the world. A horizontal relationship among the episcopal conferences could be developed by a regular pattern of official visits from conference to conference by a special delegation representing an entire conference. A reciprocal exchange of visitors would be most beneficial for episcopal conferences with common problems due to their geographical proximity, for example, the United States and Canada. But it would also be advantageous in promoting a sense of common interest and shared responsibility among episcopal conferences on different continents, for example, the South American bishops and the various African conferences.[13]

13. For a chart indicating the frequency of official "exchanges" among

3. THE CHURCH IN THE WORLD

Immense world-wide commitments await a truly international
Church. In effect the council has told mankind that the resources
of the Church are at last on the way to aid in every single
human problem.

> The Church must be clearly present in the midst of the
> community of nations, both through her official channels
> and through the full and sincere collaboration of all Chris-
> tians—a collaboration motivated solely by the desire to be
> of service to all (PCC 89).

> Those Christians are to be praised and supported, therefore,
> who volunteer their services to help other men and nations.
> Indeed, it is the duty of the whole People of God, following
> the word and example of the bishops, to alleviate as far as
> they are able the sufferings of the modern age (PCC 88).

In the matter of world peace the council did not confine its
recommendations to abstract moralizing. Instead the council
fathers specifically referred to the importance of Christian support for a universal public authority capable of enforcing peace
whenever needed.[14]

> It is our clear duty, therefore, to strain every muscle in
> working for the time when all war can be completely out-
> lawed by international consent. This goal undoubtedly
> requires the establishment of some universal public author-
> ity acknowledged as such by all and endowed with the

---

the various episcopal conferences during the Vatican Council, see Rock
Caporale, S.J., *Vatican II: Last of the Councils* (Baltimore: Helicon Press,
1964), p. 70. The U. S. episcopal conference received only three official
observers from other conferences and did not send observers.

14. "It seems to me that in the encyclical [*Pacem in Terris*] we can
discern a fourfold appeal:
   An appeal for respect for the individual.
   An appeal for collaboration among nations.
   An appeal for the creation of a supranational power.
   An appeal for collaboration among men despite their ideological
   differences"—Cardinal Suenens, *The Church in Dialogue*, p. 97.

power to safeguard on the behalf of all, security, regard for justice, and respect for rights (PCC 81).

The people of God now live in a world where science, technology, improved transportation and instant communication have established a single world community in which the rich grow richer and the poor grow poorer at an alarming rate. In this world community the love of Christ will become incarnate only when Christians are prepared to act internationally in bringing organized will and dedicated endeavor into specific projects resulting in the distribution of wealth demanded by social justice.

Christians should cooperate willingly and wholeheartedly in establishing an international order that includes a genuine respect for all freedoms and amicable brotherhood between all. This is all the more pressing since the greater part of the world is still suffering from so much poverty that it is as if Christ Himself were crying out in these poor to beg the charity of the disciples (PCC 88).

It will not be necessary to establish new organizations for this purpose. Catholic and Protestant agencies, both national and international, currently engaged in relief and technical assistance, could effectively combine efforts in a joint endeavor.

Since cooperation in social matters is so widespread today, all men without exception are called to work together; with much greater reason are all those who believe in God, but most of all, all Christians in that they bear the seal of Christ's name. Cooperation among Christians vividly expresses that bond which already unites them, and it sets in clearer relief the features of Christ the Servant. . . . It should also be intensified in the use of every possible means to relieve the afflictions of our times, such as famine and natural disasters, illiteracy and poverty, lack of housing, and the unequal distribution of wealth. Through such cooperation, all believers in Christ are able to learn easily how they can understand each other better and esteem each other more, and how the road to the unity of Christians may be made smooth (DOE 12).

The special agencies of the United Nations (as the World Health Organization, the Food and Agricultural Organization, the United Nations Educational, Scientific and Cultural Organization), which are carrying out specialized tasks in increasing food production and eliminating disease and illiteracy, could receive an effective religious dimension through efforts supplied by Christians either individually through personal commitment or organizationally through membership in an affiliated association.[15]

> They [the laity] should cooperate in a brotherly spirit with other Christians, with non-Christians, and with members of international organizations, always having before their eyes the fact that "the building up of the earthly city should have its foundation in the Lord, and should be directed towards Him" (DMA 41).

> Let Christians labor and collaborate with others in rightly regulating the affairs of social and economic life. . . . Furthermore, let them take part in the strivings of those peoples who, waging war on famine, ignorance, and disease, are struggling to better their way of life and to secure peace in the world. In this activity, the faithful should be eager to offer prudent aid to projects sponsored by public and private organizations, by governments, by various Christian communities, and even by non-Christian religions (DMA 12).

The international organizations are for today's world what the universities were for the thirteenth century; the Christian message will reach an influential part of mankind only if it has a

15. "It is our earnest wish that the United Nations Organization—in its structure and in its means—may become ever more equal to the magnitude and nobility of its tasks, and that the day may come when every human being will find therein an effective safeguard for the rights which derive from his dignity as a person, and which are therefore universal, inviolable and inalienable rights"—John XXIII, *Pacem in Terris.*

vital place at the new points of contact for organizers and developers. If the Church attempts to maintain charitable and social assistance apart from the organized efforts of men of good will, it runs the risk of losing the opportunity to meet the modern world where it is most susceptible to a meaningful encounter. Association in striving for a better world will provide Christians with both the relevance and the commitment required to convince men of the saving mission of the Church.

4. COOPERATION AMONG CHRISTIANS

Vatican II's *Declaration on the Relation of the Church to Non-Christian Religions* pays specific tribute to the great religions of the world.

> In Hinduism, men contemplate the divine mystery and express it through an inexhaustible abundance of myths and through searching philosophical inquiry. They seek freedom from the anguish of our human condition either through ascetical practices or profound meditation or a flight to God with love and trust (DOR 2).

> Buddhism, in its various forms, realizes the radical insufficiency of this changeable world; it teaches a way by which men, in a devout and confident spirit, may be able either to acquire the state of perfect liberation, or attain, by their own efforts or through higher help, supreme illumination (DOR 2).

> The Church regards with esteem also the Moslems. They adore the one God, living and subsisting in Himself, merciful and all-powerful, the Creator of heaven and earth (5), who has spoken to men; they take pains to submit whole-heartedly to even His inscrutable decrees, just as Abraham, with whom the faith of Islam takes pleasure in linking itself, submitted to God (DOR 3).

These statements were obviously intended to improve the relations of the Church to the other world religions, relations which were often quite strained in those missionary territories where Christian efforts at evangelization had failed to respect the spiritual and cultural values of those of different beliefs.

> Since in the course of centuries not a few quarrels and hostilities have arisen between Christians and Moslems, this Sacred Synod urges all to forget the past and to work sincerely for mutual understanding and to preserve as well as to promote together for the benefit of all mankind social justice and moral welfare, as well as peace and freedom (DOR 3).

The mistakes of the past are now to be corrected by deliberate efforts to promote the particular values of various cultures in cooperation with the religions of the area.

> The Church, therefore, exhorts her sons, that through dialogue and collaboration with the followers of other religions, carried out with prudence and love and in witness to the Christian faith and life, they recognize, preserve and promote the good things, spiritual and moral, as well as the socio-cultural values found among these men (DOR 2).

By cooperation with Protestant missionaries in joint efforts at providing Christian education, and by a common witness through combined medical and technical assistance, the missions have a singular opportunity to terminate the scandal of a divided Christian approach to evangelization.[16] There is also the obvious opportunity to radiate a corporate influence far superior to previous independent efforts. Cooperation among the Christian

16. "As soon as Protestantism organized its own missions, another phase began: from that time on, Christian missionaries have appeared as rivals. There have been many conversions, but hardly corresponding to the sum total of efforts and sacrifices made to send and support the missions. And this very day, when all the churches of disunited Christendom are burning with missionary zeal, we can see the handwriting on the wall. For one African convert to Christianity, ten are converted to Islam. The number of births in India each year is approximately equal to the number of Christians in that country, which is to say that Indian Christianity is, in proportion to the total population, dwindling. In China, Christianity is being wiped out"—George H. Tavard, *The Church Tomorrow* (New York: Herder and Herder, 1965), pp. 141-142.

Churches could lead to the adoption of a common profession of faith for use in a particular missionary area, and this practice would have far reaching effects toward eventual Christian unity.

> Catholics should cooperate in a brotherly spirit with their separated brethren, according to the norms of the *Decree on Ecumenism,* making before the nations a common profession of faith, insofar as their beliefs are common, in God and in Jesus Christ, and cooperating in social and in technical projects as well as in cultural and religious ones. . . . This cooperation should be undertaken not only among private persons, but also, subject to approval by the local Ordinary, among Churches or ecclesial communities and their works (DMA 15).

It is also possible that a joint commission of Protestant and Catholic missionaries could adopt a particular pattern of common worship in a missionary area which would then become an accepted part of all evangelical efforts.[17] Common worship among Christians is recognized by the council as a desired ideal in those cases (for example, Catholic and Orthodox Christians) in which the spiritual good of those involved would be a compelling reason.

> Pastoral experience shows clearly that, as regards our Eastern brethren, there should be taken into consideration the different cases of individuals, where neither the unity of the Church is hurt nor are verified the dangers that must be avoided, but where the needs of the salvation of souls and their spiritual good are impelling motives. For that reason the Catholic Church has always adopted and now adopts

17. For a comparison of Protestant-Catholic missionary strategy, see Norman A. Horner, *Cross and Crucifix in Mission* (Abingdon Press, 1965). Dr. Horner, a missionary in West Africa for ten years, compares and evaluates Protestant and Catholic missionary approaches in a variety of areas: the missionary purposes of the churches, the missionary personnel, the use of native leadership, the reaction of the missions to non-Christian environment, general and technical education, medicine and welfare. He believes that the most helpful areas for promoting Catholic-Protestant understanding in missionary activity are those in specialized activities and interests.

rather a mild policy, offering to all the means of salvation
and an example of charity among Christians, through participation in the sacraments and in other sacred functions
and things (DCC 26).

It would be profitable to consider devising suitable means by
which a practice possible among Catholics and Orthodox could
be extended to include all Christians. And cooperative efforts by
Protestant and Catholic missionaries in producing common trans-
lations of the Scriptures could lead to a common development of
the liturgical and catechetical techniques most suited to adapt
the Gospel message to its hearers.[18]

> Since the word of God should be accessible at all times, the
> Church by her authority and with maternal concern sees to
> it that suitable and correct translations are made into dif-
> ferent languages, especially from the original texts of the
> sacred books. And should the opportunity arise and the
> Church authorities approve, if these translations are pro-
> duced in cooperation with the separated brethren as well,
> all Christians will be able to use them (CDR 22).

There are many specific forms of cooperation among Christian Churches which are possible on a world-wide basis. The full
weight of Christian testimony could be brought to bear on world
problems by the practice of making united statements with the
World Council of Churches.[19] The civil rights issue offers a clas-

18. "The World Council is not only an organism in which Christians
attempt to reach closer unity, but it is also the inspirer of many worthwhile
and practical initiatives in which all churches can cooperate without
jeopardizing their beliefs. The absence of Catholics in activities that have
no dogmatic implications (such as charitable endeavors) weakens the witness of Christian charity in our non-Christian world"—Tavard, *The Church
Tomorrow*, p. 48.

19. "The gigantic forward thrust of the early Christian missions (un-
equalled by the missions of modern times, though working with the most
up-to-date techniques and with utter devotion) was based to a great
extent on the liturgy which was constantly adapted to new needs, and was
celebrated in a language which the people understood"—Hans Küng, *The
Council, Reform and Reunion* (New York: Sheed and Ward, 1961), p. 62.

sic example of how the collective voice of the entire Christian people is far more effective than statements by individual Churches. Vatican II has clearly expressed itself on the evil of discrimination.

> No foundation therefore remains for any theory or practice that leads to discrimination between man and man or people and people, so far as their human dignity and the rights flowing from it are concerned.
>
> The Church reproves, as foreign to the mind of Christ, any discrimination against men or harrassment of them because of their race, color, condition of life, or religion (DOR 5).

But would this statement be even more effective if it were jointly issued by the entire Christian leadership? A single Christian voice would be most effective in summoning world opinion to the urgent search for peace.

> The Council wishes passionately to summon Christians to cooperate, under the help of Christ, the author of peace, with all men in securing among themselves a peace based on justice and love and in setting up the instruments of peace (PCC 77).

It would also be possible to join with the World Council of Churches in planning collective attacks on hunger, poverty and population problems. Joint commissions of Protestants and Catholics could be formed to report on special problems confronting Christianity, and a common pool of Scripture and theological scholars could be formed.

> Catholic exegetes then and other students of sacred theology, working diligently together and using appropriate means, should devote their energies, under the watchful care of the sacred teaching office of the Church, to an exploration and exposition of the divine writings. . . . The sacred synod encourages the sons of the Church and Biblical scholars to continue energetically, following the mind of the Church, with the work they have so well begun with a constant renewal of vigor (CDR 23).

Combined development of their common biblical inherit-ance would unite Christians and Jews in a way in which they have not been united throughout their common history. The resulting dialogue could be the single, most effective means of terminating the anti-semitism of the past.

Since the spiritual patrimony common to Christians and Jews is thus so great, this Sacred Synod wants to foster and recommend that mutual understanding and respect which is the fruit, above all, of biblical and theological studies as well as of fraternal dialogues (DOR 4).

In the internationalization of the Church, the great religious orders have a singular contribution to make.

After considering the needs of the Universal Church and individual dioceses, they [the religious orders] should adapt them to the requirements of time and place, employing appropriate and even new programs and abandoning those works which today are less relevant to the spirit and authen-tic nature of the community (DOA 20).

Originally intended as supra-diocesan, supra-national organiza-tions, the religious orders have in many instances acquired an institutional respectability which concentrates their efforts on excessively narrow lines. Vatican II has clearly indicated what the Church now expects of religious communities.

The adaptation and renewal of the religious life includes both the constant return to the sources of all Christian life and to the original spirit of the institutes and their adapta-tion to the changed conditions of our time.

Let constitutions, directories, custom books, books of prayers and ceremonies and such like be suitably re-edited and, obsolete laws being suppressed, be adapted to the decrees of this Sacred Synod (DOA 2-3).

It is significant that in the renewal of religious orders the council established the Gospel with its universalizing tendency as the highest rule, and the original mentality of the founder as the attitude to be expected today.

> The ultimate norm of the religious life is the following of Christ set forth in the Gospels; let this be held by all institutes as the highest rule.
>
> It redounds to the good of the Church that institutes have their own particular characteristics and work. Therefore let their founders' spirit and the special aims they set before them as well as their sound traditions—all of which make up the patrimony of each institute—be faithfully held in honor (DOA 2).

Religious orders which are prepared to re-examine the Gospel and the general attitude of their respective founders can be expected to adopt a fluidity of operation permitting them to accept special commitments from either national hierarchies or the universal Church.

> Religious should consider it an honor to respond promptly and faithfully to the requests and desires of the bishops and in such a way they may assume an even more ample role in the ministry of human salvation. This they should do with due respect for the character of their institute and in keeping with their constitutions which, if needs be, should be accommodated to this goal in accord with the principles of this conciliar decree (DCP 35).

Institutes and religious houses whose small size does not permit a national or international assignment should either be incorporated into the diocesan structure or permanently joined to a larger religious organization.

> There may be communities and monasteries which the Holy See, after consulting the interested local Ordinaries, will judge not to possess reasonable hope for further development. These should be forbidden to receive novices in the future. If it is possible, these should be combined with other more flourishing communities and monasteries whose scope and spirit is similar (DOA 21).

Of course the Church can make no contribution to the international order or even to its own international mission without personnel specifically trained in various fields. A pattern of secretariats located throughout the world (as the Secretariat for Christian Religions in Geneva, the Mission Secretariat in Manila, the Secretariat for Non-Christian Religions in Bombay) could serve as great workshops where experts could periodically assemble to reassess Christian efforts. Special institutes drawing top personnel from all over the world could be regularly assembled in certain centers designed for research in particular fields (liturgy, catechetics), and their findings could be documented for universal distribution.

What the *Decree on Priestly Training* says regarding the value of special institutes for future priests could reasonably be expanded to include the training of sisters and lay leaders at international centers through special grants in aid from their dioceses.

> It will be the bishops' concern that young men suited by temperament, virtue, and ability be sent to special institutes, faculties, or universities so that priests may be trained at a higher scientific level in the sacred sciences and in other fields which may be judged opportune (DPT 18).

The various episcopal conferences could be expected to pool their efforts in establishing pastoral institutes specializing in developing apostolic techniques applicable within their own nation. It would also be understood that each episcopal conference would make its most competent personnel available for service on an international staff of general consultants, which would be available whenever their services were requested throughout the world. Associations which have made a singular contribution to Catholic life through their own initiative within a particular nation, such as the United States Liturgical Conference, could assist in the formation of an international conference with a similar pattern of free association, bringing together the skilled and the proficient from many nations.

> All associations of the apostolate must be given due appreciation. . . . Among these associations, moreover, international associations or groups of Catholics must be specially appreciated at the present time (DOL 21).

In this way the Church would acquire a staff of recognized experts, available for assignment within its own world-wide organizational pattern, who would also be prepared to represent the Church officially to international organizations and at international assemblies. A "team" concept of representation, involving a mixed delegation (one example would be a three-man delegation consisting of an African, a German and a Japanese), would be preferable to a single delegate, as a more obvious manifestation of the supra-national status of the Church.

Since the office of apostolic delegate or nuncio was established at a time when the absence of communication made personal diplomacy necessary, a situation which is obviously non-existent today, it is undoubtedly preferable to have the elected president of each episcopal conference serve as the official Church representative within a particular nation. The role of apostolic delegate to a nation's hierarchy was never intended to include the function of acting as general superintendent of the Church in that nation. In recent years certain apostolic delegates and nuncios have made valuable contributions to the Church, especially in peaceful negotiations, but the same effort and comparable success could be expected from the entire episcopacy of a nation acting through their elected president. And in the open Church of the post-Vatican II era there will be little justification for continuing the behind-the-scenes control of ecclesiastical machinery, which can be a regrettable characteristic of an appointive official without a clearly defined status. The fathers of the council indicated their desire of terminating this unfortunate practice in those areas where it now exists.

> The Fathers also desire that, in view of the very nature of the pastoral office proper to the bishops, the office of legates of the Roman pontiff be more precisely determined (DCP 9).

Once again it is important to emphasize that in the post-conciliar era the internationalization of the Church will not be an automatic process. To become truly international the Church will require the careful and detailed development of structures which both facilitate the execution of its universal mission and further encourage the development of a universal attitude. In the absence of these patterns of associationship, there could be an unintended but definite movement toward oligarchy as those closest geographically once again assumed predominance in advisory assistance to a non-consulting authority.

It is not pleasant to contemplate the consequences of a failure to make clear to the world the international nature of the Church in the post-conciliar period. A reversion to anything resembling the domestic provincialism characteristic of the pre-Vatican II management of it would be disastrous after an international council. The failure to devise structures and procedures effectively continuing the mutual exchange of views and fraternal assistance initiated by Vatican II would result in a tragic loss of energy and enthusiasm on the part of all Christians.

After years of isolation on the periphery of the decision-making apparatus of the Church it will be rather difficult for many of the laity to realize that the supposedly self-sufficient mechanisms of ecclesiastical organizations are now in need of their assistance. But it is undeniable that through Vatican II the Holy Spirit has summoned every Christian to personal involvement in the cause of Christ.

> The laity . . . should endeavor to bear witness to Christ, first of all by carrying out their individual duties or office expertly and with an apostolic spirit, and, further, by being of direct help in the pastoral activity of the Church—to the best of their ability—through their technical, economic, cultural and artistic talents (DMS 13).

If the Spirit's clearly expressed ideal of close collaboration throughout the entire Church is to become a reality, it should be evident that adroit parishioners are needed to propose workable plans for a representative direction of parish affairs. On the diocesan level, the managerial and administrative abilities of those skilled in modern organizational techniques can be used to coordinate the united efforts of thousands. Of special value to the Church will be the experience of those familiar with the techniques of international associations and conferences.

In the final analysis, the desired internationalization of structure and attitude within the Church will take place if individual Christians are determinedly international.[20]

> All nations are coming into ever closer unity. Men of different cultures and religions are being brought together in closer relationships. There is a growing consciousness of the personal responsibility that every man has (DRF 15).

A "growing consciousness" of the responsibility that each one of us has for the international order could be considered as a

20. "What can we American Catholic laymen do? First, we must begin to understand what the Church's teachings on peace and international life are all about. We must study what the popes and the bishops have said. We must develop a basic understanding of the Church's teachings on this matter.

"Second, we must make every effort to promote the understanding and consequences of these teachings among both Catholics and non-Catholics. So much depends on a widespread understanding of how we are to proceed in the cause of peace . . .

"Third, we must become personally involved in the struggle for peace and international understanding, if only in a small, minor way. . . .

"Corresponding with someone in another land, sending American books and magazines where they will do the most good, sponsoring lectures on the Church and peace in your parish or diocese, joining a group such as the Catholic Association for International Peace—the list is limited only by the imagination of the individual. . . .

"But perhaps the greatest lesson we need to learn is that international affairs and peace are no longer—if they ever were—solely the affair of diplomats. Foreign affairs are as close as the foreign student at your local educational institution. We can no longer ignore the world beyond our family circle"—Donald J. Thorman, *The Emerging Layman* (Garden City, N. Y.: Doubleday, 1962), pp. 222-224.

result of a growing consciousness of what it means to be a Christian in the world. It never was the intention of the apostles to divide the world into areas of specific responsibility for the early Christians, except as an expedient to preliminary action. Every bishop has a universal duty; every Christian bears the responsibility of bringing Christ to the world.

> Bishops should also be mindful, in administering ecclesiastical property, of the needs not only of their own dioceses but also of the other local Churches, for they are also a part of the one Church of Christ (DCP 6).

> They [the laity] should develop an ever-increasing appreciation of their own diocese, of which the parish is a kind of cell, ever ready at their pastor's invitation to participate in diocesan projects. Indeed, to fulfill the needs of cities and rural areas, they should not limit their cooperation to the parochial or diocesan boundaries but strive to extend it to interparochial, interdiocesan, national, and international fields (DOL 10).

If both individually and collectively the people of God begin to communicate their conviction of the value of a truly international Church, the upward pressure will be sufficiently intense to bring into existence the necessary structures and pattern of apostolic activity.

Chapter Six

THE DEVELOPMENT OF LEADERS: PLANNED OR UNPLANNED?

I have proposed elsewhere[1] that at the conclusion of the Vatican Council the American bishops name a commission to review the entire seminary system in the United States. This would have the double purpose of rating its efficiency and of making pertinent recommendations regarding the implementation of the conciliar decrees. But why should a survey of leadership development in the American Church be confined to a comprehensive examination of the training program provided for priests? A nationwide review (and analysis of recommendations) would be more beneficial if it were extended to include the development of leaders among the *entire* people of God, priests, religious, sisters and laity.

There might once have been point in arguing that the training given to priests, sisters and laity is necessarily different, and therefore not susceptible to collective analysis. But in recent years there has been a definite trend among seminaries and novitiates to establish houses of study on or near university campuses. There has also been a remarkable growth of institutions offering advanced training to priests, sisters and laity in a combined facility. The expected continuation of these trends

1. See Joseph O'Donoghue, "Reforming the Seminaries," *Commonweal*, November, 1964.

may produce a situation in which collective training becomes the dominant pattern in certain areas. Any hesitancy to examine our total effort on a comprehensive basis, and to make informed recommendations regarding a collective improvement of the entire training pattern, would deprive the Church of a unique opportunity to improve substantially the quality of Catholic life in the United States.

In the absence of a comprehensive review of the entire leadership development program, it could happen that major attention would be focused on the improvement of institutions training priests and sisters without similar attention being directed toward the institutes currently engaged in developing lay leaders. A frank and authoritative report on the value of the relatively small number of existing facilities for developing lay leaders would be a powerful impetus toward their expansion. A comprehensive report would also reveal possible patterns of combined training of priests, sisters and laity in centralized institutes.

In view of the council's repeated emphasis on the important place of the laity in the Church, it would seem unrealistic merely to hope for the development of a laity capable of fulfilling the ideals of Vatican II without providing high caliber training facilities. It would seem equally unrealistic to attempt to develop such institutes independently of the resources of personnel and facilities now used in the training of priests and sisters.

A cogent argument in favor of an immediate review of leadership development within the Church would be to recall the current consequences of the fact that there has never been a comprehensive analysis of the overall effectiveness of the American seminary. The absence of an authoritative report on the American seminary has meant that the seminary system must now contend with a great deal of criticism which is generally salutary in its content but which is necessarily based on fragmentary evidence.

As a reaction to abuses prevalent in the period prior to the Reformation, the Council of Trent placed heavy emphasis on the careful development of priests in special institutions separated from society.[2] Improved training was certainly a significant factor in the recovery of the Church during the counter-reformation: a disciplined, dedicated clergy was produced according to the seminary program outlined by Trent and subsequently developed by the Sulpician and Vincentian seminary directors. The rigidity of this training, the austerity of the discipline, and the isolated atmosphere may have been beneficial to the Church in the decades immediately following the establishment of seminaries. The indefinite perpetuation of these characteristics, however, produced results unforeseen and unintended by the fathers of the Council of Trent.

One result was that rigidity of training generally led to rigidity of attitude among churchmen. The seminary undoubtedly produced the dedicated and disciplined individuals for which it was frequently extolled, but the larger issue of what they were dedicated *to* and disciplined *for* was frequently determined by a narrow and decidedly unoptimistic view of the Church's place in the world.

A second result which was equally significant in the post-tridentine development of the Church (but which does not usually receive the attention it deserves) is that the tridentine pattern of seminary reform initiated a separateness of clergy and laity in their formative period which undoubtedly had repercussions in later clergy-laity relations. Before Trent those who became Church leaders had generally received their education in institutions open to all. After Trent a curious "trek to the wilderness" was inaugurated whereby seminaries and novitiates

2. For a history of seminary education from the apostolic age to the present time, see John Tracy Ellis, "A Short History of Seminary Education" in *Seminary Education in a Time of Change,* edited by James Michael Lee and Louis J. Putz, C.S.C. (Notre Dame: Fides, 1965), pp. 1-81.

attained an antiseptic isolation which ultimately influenced the clergy's general attitude toward society.

The United States seminary tended to adopt the protective isolation of its European counterpart, with some limited modification achieved through the influence of the American environment.[3] A crucial problem in its development was related to the fragmentation of resources. Canon law's directive that a seminary be established in every diocese was followed literally, with disastrous results to the overall quality of the seminary system in the United States. There were simply not enough trained spiritual directors and competent professors to staff the miniscule institutions which came into existence with obviously inadequate resources. The inevitable result of continued isolation and fragmentation of resources and personnel was that academic failings (frequent lack of accreditation, small and ill-prepared faculties, inadequate libraries, a non-intellectual atmosphere) were frequently paralleled by spiritual shortcomings such as inbred spirituality, an over-emphasis on obedience and docility, the adoption of a monastic-like withdrawal from the world and its concerns.

There were exceptions, of course, but adequately staffed and sufficiently endowed seminaries are rather rare in the United States—a fact recognized by the American bishops who in many instances preferred to send their best candidates out of their own dioceses either to a seminary associated with a university (usually Catholic University in Washington) or to an institution in Rome. The proliferation (and resulting dissipation of resources) of seminaries remains an intense problem in the American Church: over 300 new seminaries have been established since

3. For an evaluation of the historical development of the American seminary and a proposal for its modernization, see Stafford Poole, *Seminary in Crisis*. Father Poole believes that if the seminary is to keep abreast of the modern world it is going to have to be reunited organically with lay education and university life without losing its distinctive character as a professional school.

1945, each new institution putting additional strains on resources which were already in short supply.

Although the critical reassessment of Catholic higher education initiated in the mid-1950's by Monsignor John Tracy Ellis did not deal immediately with the American seminary, the intervening years have seen a steady increase in the criticism of that institution. Father Stafford Poole[4] could say in 1964 that it is now fashionable for Catholic intellectuals to look down on the training of priests with a mixture of tolerance and amused condescension. And at first glace it would seem that most of the criticism directed toward seminary training has come from lay sources. The recent evaluations of the seminary offered in the more comprehensive discussions of American Catholic life in Daniel Callahan's *The Mind of the Catholic Layman* and Michael Novak's *A New Generation* were sufficiently provocative to insure their books as long a stay on the Catholic best-seller list as that enjoyed by Thomas O'Dea's *American Catholic Dilemma,* which had appeared six years earlier.[5]

Nevertheless, less publicized but equally important evaluations have been presented in the papers and the discussions of the seminary departments of the National Catholic Educational Association. Here it seems that toleration and amused condescension are elements noticeably absent from the discussion. Father Sergius Wroblewski, O.F.M., for instance, has said:

> Generally, seminary training is too authoritarian. . . . It is content with orders and commands and human tasks that have immediate tangible results. And what is the result? The seminary rears a man incapable of assuming his sacred and human commitments, a man who very soon loses his desire of using his liberty on the plane of personal generosity.[6]

4. Stafford Poole, "Tomorrow's Seminaries," *America,* January 18, 1964.
5. See also Michael Novak, "Break with the Past," *Commonweal,* June, 1963.
6. Sergius Wroblewski, O.F.M., "Formation of Seminarians Towards a

The remarks of Father Wroblewski are an unusually straightforward (but certainly not unique) illustration of a growing tendency on the part of seminary officials to compensate for a lack of comprehensive information by rigorously reappraising the academic and moral formation value of an institution that has previously been exempt from such questioning.

It is difficult to be authentically objective in considering an institution about which so little is known with certainty, and whose widely varying pattern makes it difficult even to offer general statements on its overall effectiveness. When presented with the criticism that today's seminary is academically inadequate, excessively disciplined and inimical to personal initiative, the defender of the system can reply by citing a number of institutions that do not fall into that classification.

But the evidence that has been discovered up to this time could be considered as reinforcing the privately expressed concerns of seminary officials and the more publicized fears of the lay critics. A study made in 1959 by Father Cyril Dukehart indicated that over forty percent of American seminaries had fewer than 50 students.[7] A brief survey of the seminary entries in the 1966 Kennedy Catholic Directory reveals that there has been no significant change in this pattern. One does not need a Master's Degree in Education to appreciate the academic inefficiency in maintaining over 200 separate but similar institutions with fewer than 50 students in each.

Additional support for a critical view of seminary discipline has been supplied by the Brooks study of the adjustment prob-

---

Diocesan Spirituality," *National Catholic Educational Association Bulletin*, August, 1962, p. 78.

7. In 1959 Cyril Dukehart, S.S., reported that only eleven Catholic seminaries in the U. S. were accredited at the college level. See Fichter, *Religion as an Occupation*, p. 100 n. See also Campion Robert Baer, O.F.M.Cap., *The Development of Accreditation in American Catholic Seminaries, 1890-1961*, unpublished doctoral dissertation, Notre Dame University, 1963. On the basis of his investigation, Father Baer concluded that relatively few seminaries have obtained accreditation.

lems of 200 former major seminarians.[8] Over one-third of those interviewed reported difficulty in exercising initiative and in making decisions following their departure from the seminary. A significant number of these informants regarded this tendency as a carry-over from their previous passive reliance on seminary discipline. Thus on the basis of available evidence, it would seem that the critics who have recently attributed much of the clergy's temporizing on socio-moral issues to the fact that a number of today's clergy were trained in passively orientated institutions have raised questions which deserve serious consideration by all who are concerned about effective Christian leadership.

It should be clear that adequate answers to these questions cannot be expected to come from any individual effort. Only extensive research, conducted by professional analysts under the direction of a competent board of review, will obtain the information necessary to evaluate present efforts adequately and to improve future programs, not only in seminaries but also in novitiates for sisters and institutes for lay leaders.

Thus it would now seem extremely important for the American Church to appoint a distinguished commission of forty or fifty members who would make a comprehensive review of our national effort to develop leadership among priests, sisters and laity. The commission's goal would admittedly be enormous: to analyze the effectiveness of present efforts, and to make specific recommendations for future programs of leadership development. But the current fragmentation of programs, and the absence of factual data on their relative effectiveness—or lack of effectiveness—should make it obvious that an intense analysis is a matter of urgent importance.

To insure complete objectivity and a certain freshness of approach, the majority of commission members should not be

8. See Robert M. Brooks, O. Praem., "The Former Major Seminarian," *National Catholic Educational Association Bulletin,* August, 1961, pp. 45 ff.

institutional officials but clerics and laymen with obvious background qualifications for their assignment. It would be essential that each member of the commission be a recognized leader with a record of having assisted in the development of leaders. Clichés and generalities based on little or no experience in the leadership development field would not be particularly helpful. Considerable financial resources would be required to support the professional research teams operating on assignments from special committees of the commission. And of course the traditional reluctance of institutions and communities to release data not in keeping with their desired image would have to be somehow overcome. Religious orders and dioceses experiencing difficulties in the retention of personnel are understandably reluctant to release information regarding their problems. The assurance of anonymity and the promise of a scientific analysis useful in future planning might secure information previously unavailable.

In the *Commonweal* article previously referred to I speculated that if a seminary review commission were appointed, it would seem probable that one of its recommendations would be the removal of smaller seminaries from their widely dispersed positions and their relocation on the periphery of ten or twelve centrally located universities, whose teaching personnel and general facilities would then become available to the seminary students. This would seem to be a logical expectation in view of the fact that a number of individuals most likely to be named to the commission have previously proposed similar recommendations. On the basis of the same criterion—the commission's expected endorsement of programs either initiated or proposed earlier by its members—we can outline a few recommendations which might be offered by a commission reviewing the entire leadership development program of the American Church.

1. NATIONWIDE COORDINATION IN LEADER DEVELOPMENT

A nationwide pooling of resources in leadership development should become the accepted norm in the American Church.

There is an obvious need for bringing together resources currently fragmented in small and isolated institutions in various parts of the country. As mentioned above, a master plan of coordination would involve the closing of smaller seminaries and novitiates for both men and women and their relocation on or near the campuses of the leading universities (Catholic and secular) of the nation, whose superior faculties and resources would then be utilized in the training of future priests, sisters and lay leaders.[9]

The necessary adaptation of seminary and novitiate rules and customs to meet the variegated pattern of university life would bring the disciplinary habits of these institutions closer to the ideal of *Menti Nostrae,* a papal document directed toward the training of young men, but equally applicable to the training of sisters.

> If young men [and young women] are educated in an environment too isolated from the world, they may, in leaving the seminary [or motherhouse] find serious difficulty in their relations either with ordinary people or with the educated laity, and it may happen that they adopt a misguided and false attitude toward the faithful.

The proposed relocation would enable each community to profit by the greater academic and cultural opportunity of the university while retaining its own traditional apostolate and autonomy through continuing to maintain a form of community life while living on the university campus. The Catholic universities involved in the consolidation program would have previously recognized the high status of these students in the Church's life by agreeing to make key personnel available to the seminarians and novices. Since circumstances would necessitate a gradual program of relocation, the plan would involve no drastic allocation of the resources of the cooperating Catholic

9. Geographical proximity is in itself no guarantee of a coordination of resources. At the Catholic University of America virtually all the religious houses maintain independent theological faculties.

universities, but could become a recognized part of each university's master plan of expansion.

Similar plans of cooperation could be worked out with state universities, which in many instances have displayed a deep interest in achieving some form of association with private institutions, particularly in the field of theology. Immediate contact with the great secular universities of the nation could be expected to accelerate renewal within the Church by providing an opportunity for personal encounters and friendships within the creative centers of the modern world.

> Every means should be employed to foster suitable cooperation between Catholic schools, and between these and other schools that collaboration should be developed which the good of all mankind requires (36). From greater coordination and cooperative endeavor greater fruits will be derived particularly in the area of academic institutions (DCE 12).

The benefits derived from the latest research in those sciences which have vital implications for pastoral work (as psychology and sociology) would be immediately available to the future leaders of the Church being trained in a university milieu.

> In pastoral care sufficient use must be made not only of theological principles, but also of the findings of the secular sciences, especially of psychology and sociology, so that the faithful may be brought to a more adequate and mature life of faith (PCC 11).

State universities could offer the additional possibility of a consortium of seminaries, Catholic and Protestant, in which students would attend shared courses in various institutes.[10] Future priests, sisters and lay leaders would thus acquire a deep knowledge of other Christians, while an interchangeable Catholic-

10. A number of religious orders are in the process of combining their theological schools with the University of Chicago Divinity School.

Protestant faculty would be a powerful force in speeding efforts toward Church unity.

> Let the universities also endeavor to work together by promoting international gatherings, by sharing scientific inquiries with one another, by communicating their discoveries to one another, by having exchange of professors for a time and by promoting all else that is conducive to greater assistance (DCE 11).

The resulting theological discussions, seminars, ecumenical retreats and personal friendships would be beneficial for the laity and future sisters, but especially for future priests.[11]

> It is important that future pastors and priests should have mastered a theology that has been carefully worked out in this way and not polemically, especially with regard to those aspects which concern the relations of separated brethren with the Catholic Church. For it is the formation which priests receive upon which so largely depends the necessary instruction and spiritual formation of the faithful and of religious (DOE 10).

From Protestant students the future Catholic leaders could acquire a more intense orientation toward secular life and community affairs, while Catholic students could assist their Christian brothers in developing a sense of community based on sacramental and liturgical act.

> The circumstances of various regions being duly considered, students are to be brought to a fuller understanding of the Churches and ecclesial communities separated from the Apostolic Roman See, so that they may be able to contribute to the work of re-establishing unity among all Christians according to the prescriptions of this Holy Synod (40) (DPT 16).

11. Maryknoll seminarians and Union Theological seminarians in New York have a joint program of theological discussions, seminars and ecumenical retreats.

Intellectual formation in a university milieu could help to regain for today's priest the advanced educational position which he formerly enjoyed, but which has suffered a relative decline in recent years due to the tremendous advance in general education. On the undergraduate level, the seminarians could pursue the B.A. program in the liberal arts with majors in philosophy, history, literature or a related field, depending on the talent of the individual student. In the early stage of the plan the majority of students might be encouraged to follow the philosophy major, while a select number of students with obvious inclinations towards history or literature would be permitted to enter those fields.

A careful study of the progress of these students in their subsequent study of theology, and in their post-ordination careers, would be used to indicate whether the Church should now consider replacing its seven-century emphasis on Aristotelianism and Thomism with a wider and more comprehensive familiarity with the entire spectrum of Western thought. Since St. Thomas produced his Christian synthesis through a cultivated familiarity with the intellectual ferment of his own century and the immediately preceding century, as found in Arabic and pagan sources, we might produce another Thomas if we gave our students the same prerogative. Nineteenth- and twentieth-century thinkers, such as Hegel, Darwin, Marx and Freud, could be considerably more stimulating and beneficial as a background for theological studies than Pythagoras and his associates.

A frank and authoritative recognition by the hierarchy that the layman has a significant role to play in the training of priests and sisters should necessarily precede the actual establishment of the seminary-university consolidation. Although the majority of lay professors participating in the program would direct the study pattern and conduct seminars for the seminarians and novices in their respective fields, it is likely that there will be a steady increase in the number of laity receiving training in order to qualify as professors of theology. In addition to the many lay students doing graduate work in theology, there are at the present time over a hundred thousand former seminarians in the United States, of whom a significant number have received one or two years of theological training. There is probably an equal number of lay women who, on the basis of their previous convent life and their current professional ability, would be ideally suited to offer a distinctive contribution to the training of sisters.

The reunion lists of lay alumni and alumnae of seminaries and novitiates would seem to indicate that a significant number of these men and women enter the service professions (medicine, teaching, the Peace Corps). To this writer's knowledge no official invitation has ever been extended to them to offer their knowledge and their ecclesiastical training to the service of instructing future priests and sisters. If only one percent of those seminarians who annually leave in the second or third year of theology were to offer their gifts of dedication and motivation to the seminary, the mystical body would be considerably richer. And of course the number of laymen and laywomen who have never been in seminaries or novitiates, but who have unique gifts at developing leadership, is much higher.

At this point it might be well to consider a danger hidden in any university coordination of novitiate and seminary. In recent decades the issuance of Roman documents has been the occasion of inserting new courses in training institutes, or of expanding those in existence. The result has been a bulging curriculum which frequently pre-empts the study time necessary for the individual's personal synthesis of the course of studies. Even with these additions, most educational authorities recognize a deficiency in such fields as psychology and sociology among priests and sisters. The availability of professors on the campus who are particularly qualified in these subjects might occasion the urge to add still more courses. To avoid this development it might be advisable to declare a temporary moratorium on adding courses or hours to the curriculum, until a detailed study could be made on the effect of reducing classroom hours.

Consideration should also be given to the charge that we have been using a "funnel" theory of education in seminary and novitiate, with emphasis on classroom hours, manuals and exams, when a more personalized track system emphasizing individual study, independent investigation and seminar discussions under competent faculty direction would produce a superior product. The young priest or sister who leaves the university intensely curious about modern life, and the special problems confronting the Church in the present age, may be of greater benefit to the mystical body than the young man or woman who has methodically and deliberately acquired all the answers to all the tests.

It would be difficult to catalogue all the benefits coming to seminaries and novitiates and to the Church in general if laymen were welcomed into these institutions as teachers. A merciful end could be made to practices adopted by reason of the shortage of trained professors, such as two- and three-year cycle courses, in which both new and advanced students proceed through the same material at the same pace. Seminary and novitiate professors whose time and efforts are currently extended to teach several subjects could confine themselves to their specialty, and possibly do productive research in it.

For example, the practice of entrusting the course in Sacred Eloquence to a single instructor, who is responsible for the oratorical development of all the students during their four-year theology course, could be replaced by using a team of teachers drawn from various university departments and activities such as drama, English composition, and debating. The monotonous round of classroom lectures could be broken by seminar discussions with various professors. Students with obvious talents (writing, speaking) or with definite inclinations (liturgy, catechetics) could be placed in clinics or workshops under expert guidance.[12]

But the greatest benefit to be derived from the layman's participation in the training of priests and sisters is a benefit that cannot be catalogued or typed. Would the rapport established between lay instructor and future priest in the classroom and in seminar discussion help bridge the gulf between layman, sister and cleric? I believe it would. For too long the American layman's voice has been a voice from the periphery of our ecclesiastical world.

Appropriate financial inducements should be provided to accelerate this needed coordination of available resources.[13] Every diocese in the country could be expected to contribute annually to a common fund (possibly obtained by a national collection on a determined Sunday every year). As we have already suggested, it might be used to provide matching funds to previously separate institutions that are willing to combine facilities. For example, the funds which six or eight religious communities might raise by disposing of their miniscule training colleges (which local authorities might be willing to purchase for either a community college or a high school facility) could be equaled by an equivalent grant from the common fund designed to assist in creating a single combined institution on the borders of a university campus.[14] A distinctive community

12. For an indication of the forces of renewal currently affecting seminary life, see Lee and Putz, *Seminary Education in a Time of Change;* see also *Apostolic Renewal in the Seminary,* the papers of the Second Christopher Study Week (New York: The Christophers, 1964).

13. Immaculate Heart College of Los Angeles will become part of the vast Claremont Colleges complex when it relocates in Claremont in 1969. Seven private colleges, Pomona, Claremont Men's, Claremont Graduate, Scripps, Pitzer, Harvey Mudd and Immaculate Heart will have adjoining campuses and shared facilities.

14. An educational center pooling the resources of eight religious orders of Sisters is being established adjacent to Trinity College in Washington, D. C. Marillac College, a Sister Formation College in St. Louis, Missouri, has an enrollment of approximately 400 sisters from 31 different religious com-

life, and a number of specialized courses within the resulting
complex, would be provided to retain the distinctive apostolate
and independent action of the participating communities.

The directive of Vatican II regarding seminaries could be
applied with equal profit to institutes offering training to religious communities of men and women.

> Where individual dioceses are unable to institute their own
> seminaries properly, seminaries for many dioceses or for an
> entire region or for a country are to be set up and devel-
> oped, so that the sound training of the students, which must
> be considered the supreme law in this matter, can be taken
> care of in a more effective manner. . . .
>
> In these seminaries, however, where there are many stu-
> dents, while retaining a unity of direction and of scientific
> training, the students should be conveniently divided into
> smaller groups so that a better provision is had for the per-
> sonal formation of each (DPT 7).

It is obvious that no high school seminary or college novitiate
designed for training future priests or sisters should continue to
exist unless fully accredited by state and regional authorities.
Seminaries and novitiates without accreditation should be immediately discontinued, and their students transferred to institutions of acceptable standards. To facilitate this process, a priority scale could be established, with a special status assigned to
those programs or institutes with a definite record of leader
production. These centers would become the prime recipients of
attention and additional investment on the part of the American
Church.

It is pointless to attempt to endow equally all existing
training centers; the best institutions clearly deserve special con-

---

munities with a faculty composed of sisters from 13 congregations. Providence Heights, Issaquah, Washington and Notre Dame College, St. Louis,
Missouri, are also shared faculty institutes engaged in the education of
several communities.

sideration in the allotment of the collective resources of the American Church. There may be no possible means of preventing institutions which barely meet minimum standards from continuing to exist, but it would be helpful to have a scale by which such institutions can be recognized for what they are. On the surface this may appear to be an unduly harsh measure, but the proliferation of minuscule and understaffed training centers must somehow be arrested if the overall quality of apostolic training is to be improved.[15]

Related to the problem of pooling resources on the college level is the achievement of the same coordination on the high school level. The traditional answer in recent years to a shortage of vocations within a diocese was to build a minor seminary. In the four-year period from 1959 to 1963 one hundred and ninety new seminaries were erected, a large number of which were minor seminaries intended for high school students. It seems incredible that so much money and manpower are still being poured into this approach when the common estimate is that only 10-15 percent of these students are eventually ordained.[16]

In their total effect, many of today's minor seminaries are excellent training institutions for the 85-90 percent of their graduates who are destined to constitute the Church's laity. This is a valuable contribution to the entire life of the American Church for which sufficient credit has never been given to the dedicated priests of the high school seminary. An eventual study of the factor responsible for producing today's committed laity

15. Sister Bertrande Meyers reports that there are 93 motherhouse colleges in existence with enrollments of 55 students or less—*Sisters for the 21st Century*, p. 137.

16. A nationwide survey of the drop-out rate in U. S. seminaries conducted by Cornelius Cuyler, S.S., has indicated a steady decrease in the perseverance rate of seminary candidates. In 1939, 21.2% who completed the minor seminary reached ordination; in 1952, only 13.5% of these same students reached ordination. The perseverance rate would be considerably lower if students leaving the minor seminary prior to graduation were included—*National Catholic Reporter*, June 30, 1965.

may reveal that a most significant role was played by the minor seminary formation given in this century to over 100,000 laity.

But this valuable contribution should be recognized as such, and the institution itself re-orientated toward its actual achievement. A more effective pattern would openly recognize this result by either 1) accepting any student, boy or girl, wishing an intense spiritual and intellectual formation with the purpose of preparing for an active role in the Church, or 2) by becoming specialized institutions attached to larger high schools in which potential candidates to the priesthood or the sisterhood would have the benefit of professional counselling and spiritual formation from trained personnel. Too frequently in the past a total segregation of the sexes in training has tended to produce a segregation from life. The isolated seminary and novitiate was an innovation proposed by the Council of Trent only four hundred years ago, and thus constitutes a relatively recent development in Church life which is subject to further modification.

2. ADVANCED TRAINING FOR ALL

It is imperative that there be a lifelong formation program designed to develop the full spiritual and intellectual potential of every clerical and lay leader within the Church.

> Formation must be so organized that it takes into account the whole lay apostolate, which must be carried on not only among the organized groups themselves but also in all circumstances throughout one's whole life, especially one's professional and social life (DOL 30).

> There are many aids for lay persons devoted to the apostolate, namely, study sessions, congresses, periods of recollection, spiritual exercises, frequent meetings, conferences (DOL 32).

The *Decree on the Missionary Activity of the Church* refers to the obligation which bishops have to provide for the continuous education of the clergy.

Episcopal conferences should see to it that biblical, theological, spiritual and pastoral refresher courses are held at
stated intervals with this intention, that amid all vicissitudes
and changes the clergy may acquire a fuller knowledge of
the theological sciences and of pastoral methods (DMA 20).

Once again it would seem obvious that this ideal could best
be achieved in the United States by providing combined institutes for clerical and lay leaders. These programs would take
into account individual preferences, and would provide a professional analysis of individual talent and competency. Alternate years of training in different institutions in the United
States and overseas prior to the actual entry into the apostolate
could be supplemented by additional opportunity for training
at fixed intervals thereafter.

Adaptation and renewal depend greatly on the education
of religious. Consequently neither non-clerical religious nor
religious women should be assigned to apostolic works
immediately after the novitiate. Rather their religious and
apostolic formation, joined with instruction in arts and
science directed toward obtaining appropriate degrees, must
be continued as needs require in houses established for those
purposes. . . .
. . . Religious should strive during the whole course of their
lives to perfect the culture they have received in matters
spiritual and in arts and sciences. Likewise superiors must,
as far as this is possible, obtain for them the opportunity,
equipment and time to do this (DOA 18).

In certain cases it would be desirable that an M.A. degree
in some field replace today's B.A. degree as a requirement for
ordination or religious profession. The constantly rising level of
educational attainment in the United States will place increasing emphasis on at least a comparable level of achievement by
clergy and religious. As some form of graduate school becomes
an expected norm for the majority of college graduates, it will
be necessary for priests and sisters to work for similar advances.

The value of a graduate degree in, for example, literature, psychology or history, for a priest or a sister engaged in parish work, would not appear to be immediately evident. But in many areas it will become increasingly difficult for the Church to maintain a meaningful dialogue with the world unless its clerical and religious personnel are familiar with the contemporary issues and concerns as they are felt and expressed in literature, social studies, and so forth. A master's degree secured prior to ordination or profession would facilitate the part-time acquirement of additional academic training during the ministry.

Annual attendance at regionally located institutes offering specialized training for experienced clerical and lay leaders could become an accepted norm, while sabbatical leaves could be used for acquiring both spiritual renewal and an ever increasing knowledge at international institutes specializing in various aspects of the apostolate.

> For this purpose centers of higher institutes have been erected, and they have already proved highly successful.
> The most holy council rejoices over projects of this kind which are already flourishing in certain areas, and it desires that they may be promoted also in other areas where they may be needed. Furthermore, centers of documentation and study not only in theology but also in anthropology, psychology, sociology, and methodology should be established for all fields of the apostolate for the better development of the natural capacities of the laity—men and women, young persons and adults (DOL 32).

Lay academies established in cooperation with various Protestant Churches could offer evening and weekend courses designed to develop a common commitment through the full use of the laity in all phases of evangelical work: retreats offered to particular professions by ecumenical teams of Catholics and Protestants, inner-city programs jointly staffed by Catholic and Protestant personnel, and combined Protestant-Catholic foreign missions.

Everyone should diligently prepare himself for the apostolate, this preparation being the more urgent in adulthood. For the advance of age brings with it a more open mind, enabling each person to detect more readily the talents with which God has enriched his soul and to exercise more effectively those charisms which the Holy Spirit has bestowed on him for the good of his brethren (DOL 30).

3. ANALYSIS OF LEADERSHIP DROP-OUT

The basic personnel problem for the American Church is not the securing of additional vocations, but the retaining of vocations.[17] The much-publicized shortage of personnel is traceable in part to the high rate of loss in personnel both in the training stages (recent studies indicate that approximately 85-90 percent of the nation's minor seminary students do not complete their training) and in the subsequent ministry (by conservative estimate 10 percent of ordained clergy do not continue in the ministry). A significant step could be made toward effectively increasing the leadership force of the Church by a careful determination of the factors responsible for depletion within the ranks. It should be obvious that the equivalent of a major increase in vocations could be obtained through the removal of factors recognized as responsible for major losses, such as habits of non-consultation within communities, and local leadership unresponsive to the major needs of the Church.[18] It is pointless to direct major efforts to increasing vocations when additional gains may be more than offset by the continuation of practices resulting in a major loss of personnel. Justice would demand that

17. "The point is that the greatest difficulty in our present society is not the *finding* of vocations, but the *keeping* of them. And this difficulty increases in direct proportion to the talents and ability of the individual student"—Stafford Poole, C.M., *Seminary in Crisis*, p. 73.

18. Sister Bertrande Meyers has reported the results of one survey made by several dioceses to determine the reasons sisters give for leaving their communities. "There was one significant common denominator recorded by 95% of the cases studied: 'I did not feel that I belonged because I was neither academically nor professionally prepared for the assignment I was given in the Community's works' "—*Sisters for the 21st Century*, p. 129.

occupational hazards within the ministry (mental illness, alcoholism) be identified, and more efforts made toward reversing policies recognized as responsible for their occurrence.[19]

4. THE DEVELOPMENT OF NEW TECHNIQUES

There is a major need for specialized institutes staffed by teams of priests, sisters and laity capable of developing new techniques in different apostolates. Under the influence of centralization at university campuses, and the resultant pooling of the best leadership developing personnel, most of today's seminaries and novitiates could be expected to evolve into combined institutions capable of developing patterns of initiative and creative response to the many needs of society.

> All the forms of training, spiritual, intellectual, disciplinary, are to be ordered with concerted effort toward this pastoral end, and to attain it all the administrators and teachers are to work zealously and harmoniously together (DPT 4).

But there would remain a basic need for independent, initiative-assuming institutes capable of flexible response to varying developments within society. These specialized institutions could be located at the scene of their respective work (a Christian mission in an inner-city area, or a mission crusade centered in a factory or business complex). The institutions would be experimental centers for the development of apostolic techniques, and would provide part-time apostolic programs for those still engaged in academic preparation, thus providing a cycle of academic development, apostolic involvement, and personal reflection for future leaders.

But since it is necessary for the students to learn the art of

19. See McAllister and Vandenvelt, "Factors in Mental Illness Among Hospitalized Clergy," *Journal of Nervous and Mental Diseases,* Vol. 132 (1961), pp. 80-81. Also see the studies of Dr. John B. Wain and Sister M. William Kelley cited by Edward Wakin and Joseph F. Scheuer in "The American Nun," *Harpers,* August, 1965.

exercising the apostolate not only theoretically but also practically, and to be able to act both on their own responsibility and in harmonious conjunction with others, they should be initiated into pastoral work, both during their course of studies and also during the time of vacations, by opportune practical projects. These should be carried out in accordance with the age of the students and local conditions, and with the prudent judgment of the bishops, methodically and under the leadership of men skilled in pastoral work, the surpassing power of supernatural means being always remembered (DPT 21).

Recognition would also be given to the principle that it might be preferable for a future priest to drive a truck, join a union, work in a factory or be on his own as a salesman during his summer vacation rather than have an endless cycle of courses added to the academic year.[20] Inner-city apostolates might provide the opportunity to combine the necessary work experience with a form of apostolic commitment.

It will also be their [the bishops] charge to determine the opportuneness of providing for a certain interruption in the studies or of establishing a suitable introduction to pastoral work, in order that they may more satisfactorily test the fitness of candidates for the priesthood (DPT 12).

5. ESTABLISHING OPPORTUNITIES TO EXERCISE LEADERSHIP

The current situation in which opportunities for individuals to exercise leadership and initiative within the Church occur only after many years of subordination should be altered to permit younger leaders to work either individually or as shared-authority teams in particular programs requiring personnel initiative. Various apostolates could be so structured that all participants

---

20. Seminarians and ministers at Chicago's Urban Training Center for Christian Mission are sent out with $8.00 to live and work for four days in the slums surrounding the center's headquarters on Ashland Avenue. Cf. *Time*, November 17, 1965, p. 124.

either share in a rotation of directing positions, or simultaneously share in a group pattern of challenge and response to the Church's needs. The elective process would be widely used to determine leaders capable of unifying the charismatic gifts of all, and each position of authority would be recognized as a temporary service accepted for the benefit of the entire Church.[21] The life-long occupancy of positions of authority can tend to produce certain psychological characteristics of dominance and supposed wisdom which prevent the role of authority from being seen as one of love and service to all. Rotation in office would certainly be an aid in implementing the mentality desired by Vatican II.

> Superiors, as those who are to give an account of the souls entrusted to them (Heb 13:17), should fulfill their office in a way responsive to God's will. They should exercise their authority out of a spirit of service to the brethren, expressing in this way the love with which God loves their subjects (DOA 14).

The various apostolates would frequently utilize task forces composed of members from various communities and organizations temporarily associated for a particular assignment. Instead of operating out of the traditional conclaves of rectories, convents and other institutional headquarters, Christian leaders would operate in teams at strategic points such as university dormitories, apartment complexes, and industrial areas.

> The apostolate in the social milieu, that is, the effort to infuse a Christian spirit into the mentality, customs, laws,

21. "For the continuous training and perfecting of Superiors . . . one must not exclude the younger nuns from office, must not make conditions not made by Canon Law, not persist in re-electing the same persons, for the Church's mind is that the law and constitutions of the congregation should be obeyed and they find it good that there should be alternation in the office of Superior so that Superiors shall not be deprived of the benefits of obedience"—Sacra Congregatio de Religiosis, *Acta et Documenta Congressus Internationalis Superiorissarum Generalium*, 1952, p. 271. Quoted in Cardinal Suenens, *The Nun in the World*, p. 159.

and structures of the community in which one lives, is so much the duty and responsibility of the laity that it can never be performed properly by others. In this area the laity can exercise the apostolate of like toward like. It is here that they complement the testimony of life with the testimony of the word. It is here where they work or practice their profession or study or reside or spend their leisure time or have their companionship that they are more capable of helping their brethren (DOL 13).

6. RESEARCH IN THE APOSTOLATE

It is essential that sufficient emphasis be placed on the constant need for research and experimentation to insure a maximum return for the expenditure of apostolic energy and resources. This will require directing the necessary funds into continual research, involving careful comparison of existing programs and the use of pilot projects to determine further advances. Serious questions need to be asked and factual answers obtained before additional outlays of talent and capital are made. For example:

1. Has the American Church placed too much emphasis on the minor [high school] seminary as a tool in the formation of priests? Are the 10-15 percent of its graduates who are eventually ordained superior to priests who entered the seminary following high school? Or could the enormous investment of priest personnel currently engaged in training high school seminarians be more efficiently utilized in the development of *all* leaders, clerical and lay?

2. What are the major factors responsible for the high drop-out rate among priests and sisters? Do religious communities and dioceses where self-initiative in the apostolate and the widest use of individual talent are the expected practice have a greater initial appeal for potential candidates and a better record of retaining personnel than other communities and dioceses where these same factors are not as evident?

3. What specific techniques have proved beneficial in fulfilling the norm of Vatican II?

An effective renewal and adaptation demands the cooperation of all the members of the institute. . . . Superiors should
take counsel in an appropriate way and hear the members
of the order in those things which concern the future wellbeing of the whole institute (DOA 4).

4. What are the basic motivation patterns of young persons aspiring to a life of service in the Church? What incentives
to leadership are most effective in securing personnel with the
best natural and spiritual endowments?

Only intensive research will provide reliable answers to
these and other vital questions. Up to now the hierarchy has
been curiously reluctant to make the financial investments necessary for depth study of its problems. But the millions needed for
research projects would represent only a minuscule share of the
capital already involved in institutional architecture. It would
seem that research should have priority over further construction.

Of course, research would have to be assisted by experimental programs offering bases of comparison. For example,
scholastic philosophy is not an essential pre-requisite to theology; other major electives such as history and literature might
provide a better major field for undergraduate students preparing for leadership as priests or sisters in the Church. In theological studies, an initiation into the mysteries of Christ along
biblical, liturgical and pastoral lines could be followed by a
study of biblical themes (the idea of creation, the idea of
redemption, the prophetic office), and eventually culminate in
an independent, faculty-assisted study of the more profound,
more difficult problems of philosophy and theology.

In revising ecclesiastical studies the aim should first of all be
that the philosophical and theological disciplines be more
suitably aligned and that they harmoniously work toward
opening more and more the minds of the students to the
mystery of Christ. . . . After a suitable introduction they
are to be initiated carefully into the method of exegesis; and
they are to see the great themes of divine revelation and to

receive from their daily reading of and meditating on the
sacred books inspiration and nourishment (DPT 14, 16).

A careful study of the progress of students in their post-ordination or post-professional careers would be used to indicate the
relative merits of different methods of formation.

Teaching methods are to be revised both as regards lectures, discussions, and seminars and also the development
of study on the part of the students, whether done privately
or in small groups (DPT 17).

7. PROFESSIONAL APPROACH TO VOCATIONS

*The fragmented pattern of current recruitment efforts should be
replaced by coordinated programs presenting leadership opportunities in the Church to the widest possible audience.*[22]

The Synod moreover orders that the entire pastoral activity
of fostering vocations be methodically and coherently
planned and, with equal prudence and zeal, fostered by
those organizations for promoting vocations which, in
accord with the appropriate pontifical documents, have
already been or will be set up in the territory of individual
dioceses, regions or countries. Also no opportune aids are
to be overlooked which modern psychological and sociological research has brought to light (5).
The work of fostering vocations should, in a spirit of
openness, transcend the limits of individual dioceses, countries, religious families and rites (DPT 2).

An unfortunate side effect of the proliferation of minor seminaries was that the ever-increasing number of institutions exclusively directed toward the post-grade school clientele has centered vocation recruitment efforts around that particular age

22. For an analysis of the worldwide vocation situation, see *Today's
Vocation Crisis*, a summary of the studies and discussions at the First
International Congress on Vocations to the States of Perfection in Rome,
December 10-16, 1961, translated and edited by Godfrey Poage, C.P.,
and Germain Lievin, C.SS.R. (Westminster: Newman, 1962).

group, leaving relatively little energy or actual attention to recruitment among college students.[23] The previously mentioned formation of apostolically oriented groups on university campuses could provide a promotional effort in an area almost wholly neglected by the traditional recruitment methods.

Scattered efforts at vocation publicity programs should be assisted by establishing central information centers offering comprehensive information on all apostolates. These centers would also be equipped to provide a professional analysis of every volunteer's talent and inclinations to determine the particular commitment within the Church best suited to his ability and inclination. Since personal contact with the clergy and religious is often considered to be the most important factor in fostering vocations, the current emphasis on pamphlets and brochures would be replaced by living contact both within the apostolate (any interested person would be invited to share the day-to-day life of priests, sisters and committed laity for several days) and within the neighborhood (professed religious would frequently return to their home area to relate experiences on an informal basis).

> Religious should remember there is no better way than their own example to commend their institutes and gain candidates for the religious life (DOA 24).

The practice of having all the priests and sisters from a particular parish return annually to the parish for a public renewal of their Christian dedication would be a beneficial manifestation of the contribution which the entire community is called upon to make to Christian leadership.

23. A survey completed in June, 1965, in which 60 dioceses participated, indicated a 7% drop in seminary enrollments from the previous year. Msgr. Vincent J. Howard, vocation director of the Archdiocese of Detroit and conductor of the survey, reported that the vocation drop off was most severe in the high school seminaries—*National Catholic Reporter,* June 30, 1965.

> It will be very useful, provided the universal scope of mission work is not thereby neglected, to keep in contact with missionaries who are from one's own community, or with some parish or diocese in the missions, so that the communion between the communities may be made visible, and serve for their mutual edification (DMA 37).

Frequent contact with family members and the retention of the family name by religious would help to remove the sense of apartness felt so deeply by families of religious; a simplified habit and the occasional use of informal clothes could similarly reduce apartness within society.[24]

> The religious habit, an outward mark of consecration to God, should be simple and modest, poor and at the same time becoming. In addition it must meet the requirements of health and be suited to the circumstances of time and place and to the needs of the ministry involved. The habits of both men and women religious which do not conform to these norms must be changed (DOA 17).

8. EQUALITY FOR WOMEN IN THE CHURCH

Justice requires that the opportunity to exercise leadership in the Church not be confined to the half of the membership that is male. For women this will mean active participation in liturgical functions, full consultation in the overall planning of the Church, and complete representation on all commissions or councils that seriously affect their status and interests.[25]

24. "In 428, Pope Celestine I upbraided Honoratus, abbot of Lerins, who had been appointed bishop of Arles, for introducing a special dress, namely, the tunic and belt. This was the monastic habit and an innovation. Hitherto, priests' dress was exactly the same as that of other men. Even in the celebration of the liturgy they merely wore clean clothes. Celestine wrote to the bishops of the Narbonne province: 'We should be distinguished from others, not by our dress but by our knowledge, by our conversation, not by our manner of life' (Epistle 4; 1, 2 in *PL* 50, 431)"— Yves Congar, O.P., *Power and Poverty in the Church*, p. 57.

25. See Sidney Cornelia Callahan, *The Illusion of Eve* (New York: Sheed and Ward, 1965): "The essence of my case is adherence to a bal-

It would also mean that the privilege extended to the Missionary Sisters of Madre Laura in Columbia, to distribute Communion to the faithful, be extended to provide women with the opportunity to serve the Church as deaconesses, preaching and administering certain of the sacraments. It will also involve an objective consideration of the possibility of the ordination of women, a possibility clearly recognized by St. Joan's international alliance, which has submitted a petition to the papal commission for revising canon law. They are requesting that women be permitted to preach wherever this privilege is granted to laymen, and that they be admitted to the sacred deaconate, and eventually to the priesthood. St. Paul's frequently quoted remarks apparently banning any official ecclesiastical activity by women ("women should keep silent in the Churches for it is not permitted them to speak. . . ." [1 Cor 14:34-35], and "I do not allow women to teach or to exercise authority over men; and she is to keep quiet. . . ." [1 Tim 2:11-13]) may have been directed to particular circumstances in the primitive Church and need not necessarily be of universal and perpetual application. As Karl Rahner has indicated:

> It may not be taken for granted as certain that what the early Church did must always and in every instance be able to be done by the later Church; in other words, a decision of the primitive Church may never become an absolute for all later times and thus be considered as of Divine Law.[26]

It would seem obvious that the exclusion of women deeply interested in religion from active participation in ecclesiastical functions is contrary to the good news of Christ that every

---

anced ideal which gives freedom to different women to do different things. . . . for different women maturity can mean different things. My whole argument . . . has been just this: that the Christian freedom of women is not limited because of their sex. The feminine sex has no ready-made vocation."

26. *The Church and the Sacraments* (New York: Herder and Herder, 1964).

human being bears the likeness of God, and that each and every Christian is a child of God. The *Constitution on the Church* has established the possible criteria for considering the ordination of women:

> The chosen People of God is one: "one Lord, one faith, one baptism," sharing a common dignity as members from their regeneration in Christ; having the same filial grace and the same vocation to perfection; possessing in common one salvation, one hope and one undivided charity. There is, therefore, in Christ and in the Church no inequality on the basis of race or nationality, social condition or sex, because "there is neither Jew nor Greek; there is neither bond nor free: there is neither male nor female. For you are all 'one' in Christ Jesus" (CC 32).

What would be the overall effect of this type of report? It should be obvious that the mere reporting of the current status of leadership development by a national commission, and the corresponding presentation of its recommendations, would not be productive in itself. To be effective it would require an emphatic endorsement on the part of the entire episcopate of the United States, and a specific decision by the entire American Church to begin its implementation.

But it would seem likely that a special report of a distinguished commission would arouse the collective force of public opinion necessary to inspire unified action and eventually to produce the desired nation-wide coordination of efforts.

The Church in the post-conciliar era will make great demands of its clerical and lay leaders. Only an intense preparation collectively provided by the entire people of God can meet the legitimate expectations of a world opinion that regards the conciliar documents as a promise of a better future of mankind, and that turns to Church leadership to fulfill its expectations. The Church in America can produce such leaders if all its members are called upon to contribute their vision and their talent in an effort utilizing the ability and the resources of all.

Chapter Seven

THE FUTURE:
COURAGE OR CAUTION?

It is somewhat paradoxical that in recent centuries the Church militant has been in practice the Church cautious. Placed on the defensive by the Reformation and by the subsequent revolutionary movements within society, the Church has been extremely reluctant either to innovate or to adapt itself to what it regarded as a hostile environment. Innovation has usually been the last response to a desperate situation rather than an optimistic effort to pioneer a new approach in the apostolate.

One result of the siege mentality of the post-reformation era has been the instilling of habits of caution deep within the organizational patterns and operational mentality of the Church. In the course of the four centuries since the Council of Trent we have acquired an almost canonized pattern of docility and obedience that can be expected to continue to affect future judgments and attitudes for some time, despite the official reversal of past attitudes by the Council.[1]

It is a difficult process for an institution to begin to act con-

1. "So we must have the courage (for this can be the precise function given by the Spirit to a particular member of the Church) to say no in the Church, to make a stand against certain trends, even before the official hierarchy has been alarmed. In fact, such a protest can be God's means of rousing his ministers to act"—Karl Rahner, S.J., quoted in the *St. Louis Review,* June 18, 1965.

trary to the habits acquired through several centuries. But somehow the inherited hierarchy of virtues must be radically altered.
It is obvious that Church life in these days of the second Pentecost requires not the caution of the disciples locked in the upper
room, but rather the exhilerating courage of these same disciples after the first Pentecost. That courage triggered the Church
to an expansive effort of amazing proportions. A similar advance
can be expected from a second infusion.

Fundamentally, the new courage will be based on the
Church's conviction that through the council the Holy Spirit has
spoken to us in confidence-inspiring terms, and that the same
Spirit will now supply a charismatic power to every Christian
who is committed to the execution of its message. Pentecostal
courage will take various forms in response to the various needs
of the Church. Its display can be expected in those areas where
Christians are prepared to sacrifice habits of purely human stability in favor of a deeper reliance on the Spirit.

Initially we will need the *courage to be insecure*. The Church
has been called upon to move from the comfortable situations
of its buildings and its institutions into the uncertainty of an
unknown territory. The people of God may be as reluctant now
to leave the security of their previous practices as their ancestors
were to leave the security of Egypt. But a truly pilgrim Church
must be willing to accept the insecurity of a traveler moving
through a changing world to a promised land.

Subjectively, this will mean a loss of inner placidity as individual Christians search for forms of Christian response and
social commitment radically different from previous practice.
A divine discontent will replace the peace of mind and inner
consolation desired by the more self-centered spirituality of an
earlier age. Objectively, it will involve a willingness to analyze
honestly the actual situation in which the Church finds itself,
our accomplishments and our failures, our resources and our

inadequacies. It will require courage to collect data and to *publish* the results even when highly unfavorable. Deficiencies can no longer be regarded as minor aberrations to be hushed up by repeating the traditional clichés about our past accomplishments.

The results of courageous efforts to reappraise the Church may involve a loss of some self-esteem as we replace platitudes by a realistic look at past and present failures. We may come to realize that up to now our missionary efforts have not been spectacularly successful in a non-European world, a fact possibly attributable to our superior attitude regarding our own cultural and national inheritance, with a resulting reluctance to adopt the message to hearers not possessing our own distinctive background.[2] Perhaps our earlier policies and attitudes are as responsible for the de-Christianization of society as the forces of materialism and secularism which we traditionally castigate. We may find that our full Churches on Sunday mornings do not constitute an authentic proof of our success.[3]

But insecurity can be the beginning of wisdom. The neat formulas and the tidy solutions to all problems which made us feel so secure in the past may have had an inhibiting effect on a truly Christian response to a world of infinite complexity. Dependence on institutions and rigid organizational patterns

2. "The Church of Jesus Christ, taken as a whole, has remained a European-American affair. We might adduce several causes for this sad and disconcerting fact. But it cannot be disputed that much of the fault lies with an increasingly closed and fixed immobility in the Church (and in her missionary methods) which develops as time goes on. Indeed, it has been so in Europe too. Despite ever-increasing secularization, the Church has not been, during her second millenium, the intellectual avant-garde, as she was, on the whole, during her first thousand years"—Hans Küng, *The Council, Reform and Reunion*, p. 18.

3. Eugene J. Schallert, S.J., Professor of Sociology at the University of San Francisco, conducted a survey of 20,000 Catholics in 12 areas of California and Arizona. He found that although Catholic churches in California and Arizona are always crowded, only 28% of Catholics go to Church on Sunday. See *op. cit.*, p. 100, *supra*.

A diocesan-wide survey of the Episcopal Church of Chicago revealed that one out of every four adult Episcopalians is a former Catholic. See *Chicago Studies*, Vol. 3, No. 1, a periodical edited by the faculty of St. Mary of the Lake Seminary, Mundelein, Illinois.

can be an impediment to Christians who have here no lasting home, and whose ultimate reliance must rest on the life of the Spirit.

The courage to be insecure has been a distinctive characteristic of the founders of the great religious orders and of the truly charismatic Church leaders of every century. Their followers may not always have retained the same sense of courage—the life-giving innovations of one century tend to harden in subsequent centuries—but courage in the Spirit remains as the ideal among the people of God rather than the nerveless acceptance of what is.

We will also need the *courage to listen.* It is so much easier to be a speaking Church, a Church which directs an incessant monologue to its followers and to the world. A listening Church will hear unpleasant observations. The individual Christian will frequently present the official Church with a charismatic comment or accomplishment which challenges the accepted wisdom. The critic with his probing analysis, and the innovator with his tendency to minimize past accomplishments, will be accepted and utilized only by those who really believe in a Church "always in need of reform," who are prepared to accept the unlimited distribution of charismatic gifts within the Church as part of the Spirit's endowment to every Christian.

It has generally been difficult for the official Church to realize that it is always in need of prophetic and critical voices. The frequently irritating observations of the divinely dissatisfied are rarely accepted as a providential goad to the humanness of the Church. A supersensitivity to criticism on the part of those in authority has had disastrous effects on the life of the Church in the past. Only a listening Church will possess the characteristic insights and the secular expertise of the faithful.[4]

4. "At the Council of Jerusalem we find strong emphasis laid on what the many had to say. The Bible is not in the least ashamed to say that within the apostolic group itself there were considerable disputes. And what finally issues from this first Council is a *resolution* to whose emer-

Whether or not the Church is willing to become a listening Church may depend on the quality of its faith. Do we really and sincerely believe what the New Testament so obviously indicates: that the Spirit bestows charismatic gifts upon lay members and the lower clergy, upon nuns and brothers, by which they are enabled to see what authority does not see? Do we really trust the people of God, their good sense, their faith, and their power of judgment?

One measure of our response will be determined by our willingness to accept the prophetic role of the press. Its editorials, its articles and its letters to the editors will constitute a prime opportunity for the listening Church to measure and to apply the various gifts of this Spirit. In Catholic papers and periodicals there is a readily available forum for a constant and open debate about the directions and the effectiveness of the Church in its pursuit of goals. The press will have, as Pope Paul has indicated, the function "of prodding the inertia of those who are reluctant to adapt themselves to the course."[5]

A listening Church will not diminish the effectiveness of the teaching office. Churchmen who have learned the views and opinions of the faithful will be both better endowed and better supported in their exercise of the true role of teacher. The courage required to listen can be expected to intensify the courage needed to speak out on difficult issues.

And we will need the *courage to accept tension*. In an age of transition and rapid growth tension will be inevitable—and even

---

gence the Apostles, the presbyters and the whole community have contributed"—Hans Küng, *The Council, Reform and Reunion*, p. 136.

5. "The Pope underscored the importance of his exhortation when he chided the Italian press for its slowness in reporting it . . . Pope Paul also pointed to the need for 'prodding the inertia of those who are reluctant to adapt themselves to the course; restraining on the other hand the intemperance of others . . .' "—Papal Address in St. Peter's, *The Pope Speaks*, November, 1965.

desirable—between those deeply conscious of a deposit to be preserved and those emphasizing a relevance to be established.[6] Both views are necessary to balance one another in the determination of policy. Only through their direct confrontation will each position receive its due. As Pope John has remarked, "We are not friars singing in choirs." The customary placidity will be gone as we collectively and painfully abstract the permanent core of Christianity from its European environment and adapt it to a new world situation. The transition of Christianity from a European base into a non-European international setting may be as personally disturbing to the faithful and as traumatic to the Church as Christianity's original transfer from its Judaic origin to the Roman world. The tensions displayed in the Pauline epistles are to be again expected. The old comfort in the use of fixed techniques will also be gone as we experiment with novel and untried forms of apostolates. The acceptance of calculated risks will lead to some failures and some successes. The resulting increase of tension will need to be balanced by an increased courage in the Spirit.

The tension will be a painful experience for many. There will be pain because some persons will have an insight into the need for change long before action can be taken in that regard. On the other hand, the change when it does come will bring pain because others will not have experienced this same insight, and only gradually will they come to realize the necessity for the change. But changes which are simply legislated from the top without tension, without ferment, and without agitation are unduly susceptible to failure, because of the failure to produce

6. "We should not hesitate to affirm that much of the healthy tension in the Church today is rooted in the sensitivity of one part of her members to 'the deposit to be preserved' and in the sensitivity of another part to 'the talent to be developed.' Just as the first group puts the stress on the perennial element, the second emphasizes the dynamic. And both groups are in the right. Both groups have tasks to perform today within the one and only Church"—Cardinal Suenens, *The Church in Dialogue,* p. 40.

an environment capable of sustaining what is changed. Without previous tension and discussion, the traditional pattern can reassert itself even after the most emphatic legislative decisions on behalf of the change.

Prior to Vatican II the accepted ideal was that there be no official divergences of opinion within the Church; the tension-producing voice of dissent was regarded as suspect. The new situation requires that the no-sayer be recognized and appreciated as a beneficiary to the Church. His voice may or may not indicate the eventual decision which the Church will adopt, but without the benefit of his comment the eventual decision would be deprived of a vital factor in the preliminary dialogue. Cardinal Suenens has remarked that whereas authority has a right to the last word, the faithful have a right to the second last word. The second last word of the faithful will be heard only when the Church has the courage to accept willingly the tension involved in hearing it publicly.

Finally, we will need the *courage to dream*. It is so much easier to dismiss possible adaptations or innovations with over-worked references to past failures. An initial cynicism can cripple the potential results of even the most promising of new efforts. The traditional posture of the post-reformation Catholic was to look backward to past glories which were to be rigidly preserved. The conditioned acceptance of a disunited Christendom and a world opposed to Christian permeation and influence are psychological characteristics which will be changed only with difficulty. It will require a distinct type of courage to visualize a Christian world with all mankind united to Christ, and to direct both the personal and collective resources of the Church toward that goal. Without the courage of great vision the desired efforts will not even be initiated.

Christians may now have more reason to dream of great accomplishments than at any other time in the entire history of the people of God. Christianity within the first century of its existence accomplished an amazing missionary feat. In that effort every traveler was a bearer of the Christian message. A spirit of adaptation to local environment was followed, and evangelical fervor came from the many sources encouraging an initiating response to the various needs of the early Churches.

A similar situation prevails as Christianity begins the century of Vatican II. The conciliar recognition of the role of the laity means that every person is once again recognized as a bearer of the Christian message. The council has officially endorsed a spirit of adaptation and relevance characteristic of the apostolic Church. The evangelical fervor of thousands has been aroused, promising initiative and mutual assistance in world-wide efforts.[7]

Under favorable conditions, the vast energy now available for a dramatic Christian resurgence can constantly be increased. The benefits derived from almost a century of both Catholic and Protestant scholarship in making available our common heritage of Scripture and liturgy will undoubtedly continue. A new attitude of cooperation among Protestants and Catholics indicates a vast potential of united mission effort to correct the fragmented approach of the past. There is now both a theoretical recognition of the role of the laity in Church efforts, and the promise of practical acceptance of that involvement by millions. The courage—and the inspiration—to dream will be the great prompter to Christian commitment; the charismatic, inspired vision of potential accomplishment will be the great sustainer of every form of commitment to the modern world.

7. "We must give the life of the Church *new attitudes of mind, new aims, new standards of behaviour,* make it rediscover a spiritual beauty in all its aspects; in the sphere of thought and word, in prayer and methods of education, in art and canon law. A unanimous effort is needed in which all groups must offer their cooperation"—"Faith, Unity, and Peace: Pope Paul's Epiphany Message from Bethlehem," *The Tablet,* CCXVIII (11 January, 1964), p. 53.

Would it be chauvinistic to say that the American Church has a distinct contribution to make to the future of Christianity? Nowhere else in the world is a successful implementation of Vatican II as likely—or as possible—as it is in the United States. The collective resources of the American Church would seem to exceed that of any other Church. It has a spiritual zeal of immense proportions, a close bond between clergy and laity, and a history of great accomplishments in spreading Catholicism.[8] Equally important are the resources of the American mentality: a tradition of initiative unhampered by devotion to past customs, a habit of utilizing collective energy through adroit organizational patterns, a sense of social responsibility and the need for personal commitment. One of the great problems facing the post-conciliar Church—the utilization of all the resources of talent and energy possessed by the faithful in the great work of the Spirit—may be particularly susceptible to a precedent-setting American solution.

The theology of what the Church should be, the pattern it follows in the attainment of its mission, and the structures it utilizes to coordinate its efforts are now in a fluid state which has not been experienced for several centuries, and which may not be re-experienced for several centuries to come. It is rather painful to visualize the future consequences of a failure at this time in formulating and establishing the mentality and the procedures capable of implementing the new realization of what the Church should be. A successful effort now would mean that the people of God would enter the third millenium with an impact

8. "Numbering forty-three million or more souls and thus constituting the third largest group of Catholics anywhere in the world, by the gift of divine Providence and their own dedicated labors, the richest body of the faithful within the universal Church, and steeped in more than three centuries of practice in the veneration and love they have manifested for their clergy and for the Church, the Catholic laity of the United States constitute a vibrant and moving force in the realm of the spirit that has not been excelled in modern times"—John Tracy Ellis, *Perspectives in American Catholicism* (Baltimore: Helicon, 1962), pp. 81-82.

similar to that with which they entered their first millenium. The formation of habits of flexible response to problems, and of maximum coordination of energy and talent to various apostolates, would be a unique gift to the Church for centuries to come. It may influence Church growth and development for a period considerably longer than the four hundred years influenced by Trent. To this task of staggering dimensions each Christian is called by the Spirit to contribute his personal commitment.

In the post-conciliar era each Christian's commitment will involve participation, expression of his thoughts and his suggestions in the life of his local Church, and a contribution of his wisdom and skill in assisting the collective efforts of the Church in his diocese and in its world-wide efforts. An intense preparation and development of his own natural ability and the development of his spiritual life will be followed by some form of evangelical commitment in connection with his occupation or profession. He will clearly understand that the Holy Spirit has provided guidelines of reform and renewal through conciliar documents, and that the same Spirit continues to provide general directives through the hierarchy. But he will also realize that the implementation of what the Spirit wishes will be achieved through individuals, in virtue of the unique charismatic gift bestowed upon each.

In the last analysis, the future renewal of the Church depends on each individual Christian's theological awareness of his own charismatic endowment. If reform is to be universally effective throughout the Church, each person's charism must be recognized as God's call to that individual for a specific service within the community, and the God-given endowment of the ability to perform that service. This was the initial form of Christian response to the message of Christ as announced by the first pope: "According to the gift that each has received administer it to one another as good stewards for the manifold grace of God" (Pet 1:4-10). St. Paul also individualized responsibility:

"Each one has his own gift from God, one in this way and another in that" (1 Cor 7:7), and "The manifestation of the Spirit is given to everyone for profit" (1 Cor 12:7).

Vatican II will succeed if each of us can attain the personal conviction that *together we are the Church,* and that what each one of us believes and does ultimately affects the entire effort of Christ's redemptive work in the world. Reform, renewal, the Christianization of the universe await thousands of individual decisions and efforts in parishes, in dioceses, in the nation and in the world.